PIERCING TONGUES

Decoding The Mysteries of The Baptism of The
Holy Spirit and Speaking In Tongues

Paul Manning

Table of Contents

Preface

It was a late-fall day in 1989. I was working on a class assignment in one of my engineering classes at Virginia Tech when my telephone rang. "Hello," I answered.

"Brother Paul, what are you up to?" responded the excited voice on the other end of the line. It was my friend Bob. He and I had met at a campus ministry meeting a year earlier.

"Oh, just relaxing a bit before I dive back into studying," I replied. Bob went on to tell me that he and some mutual friends were going to a weekend retreat within the next few days to hear teachings about Christian discipleship and the baptism of the Holy Spirit—and to learn how to go to new levels of power in ministry. At that time, I had been a Christian for about three years. Having heard many conflicting teachings about the topic of the baptism of the Holy Spirit over the years, I decided to go on the retreat to learn more. This was the beginning of my journey in learning about the baptism of the Holy Spirit and the outward manifestation and evidence of this baptism, which is taught to be—speaking in tongues.

A little over two years after the retreat (January 28, 1991), I began chronicling my experiences and learnings that have led to the writing of this book. My initial confusion was followed by prayerful research, study, contemplation, and conviction by the Holy Spirit.

God has now prepared me to share my understanding of these profoundly important yet often confusing topics.

My goal in writing this book is to present clear and understandable answers to people's many questions about these confusing and divisive topics—from a solidly biblical and unbiased stance. Producing clear and consistent "Now I get it!" responses in the hearts and minds of my readers is the desired outcome of this book. Most importantly, I want to usher my readers into a closer walk with the Lord Jesus Christ. The Bible alone has been the driving source of this book's content so that readers will have only God's Word—line upon line and precept upon precept [Is. 28:10]—shedding light on dark areas of understanding and unlocking the mysteries around the topics of the baptism of the Holy Spirit and speaking in tongues.

Sadly, many people who proudly discuss what they believe about the baptism of the Holy Spirit and speaking in tongues are not biblically sound in either their personal understanding or their public exhortations. Most people I've talked with over the years about the baptism of the Holy Spirit and speaking in tongues chose what they believe based on the influence of their parents/family, the church in which they were raised or attended, or other Bible teachers who had influenced them either in person or through television, radio, or online. None of these are legitimate influences in leading someone to a proper understanding of the baptism of the Holy Spirit and speaking in tongues. Rather, only the unencumbered reading and contextual acceptance of God's Word can give us a true understanding of any doctrine—Holy Spirit baptism and speaking in tongues included.

God definitely wants us to know his reasons and purposes behind these gifts. If he did not, he would not have allowed them to be cemented into the pages of the Old and New Testaments. The intent of this book is to share the power, freedom, and truth of these teachings with you.

Introduction

A cts and I Corinthians are the two books of the Bible primarily referred to when most people research or discuss incidents in the Bible pertaining to the baptism of the Holy Spirit and speaking in tongues. Therefore, we will thoroughly explore these two books to decode the abundance of information about these two topics. Additionally, and equally important, we will examine the rest of the Scriptures from Genesis to Revelation to contextualize, substantiate, and screen our beliefs so that God's truth about these topics will shine like a beacon in our hearts, minds, and day-to-day living.

The desired outcomes of this book's analysis of the baptism of the Holy Spirit and speaking in tongues are to (1) provide readers with a clear, easy-to-understand, and thorough examination of the Scriptures regarding these topics, (2) enable followers of Christ Jesus to walk in the deeper supernatural power that God has for us by way of his indwelling Spirit, and (3) equip believers to lovingly, biblically, and confidently share with others God's truth regarding these often polarizing topics.

This study will use the Bible to inform, interpret, and answer itself. No concepts presented will rest on phrases such as "I feel…" or "It's my opinion that…" The Bible alone is the authoritative foundation on which we must doctrinally (truthfully) stand; all other ground is sinking sand. It is of utmost importance to understand that every verse in the Bible has only one interpretation—God's interpretation. While there may be different applications of God's Word in believers' lives during various times and circumstances, there is always only one contextual meaning of his Word.

If you have begun to read this book, your interest in these topics is evident. I encourage you to be prepared to let go of preconceived notions, others' beliefs, and denominational teachings that you discover are not aligned with *God's interpretation*. While it may initially feel uncomfortable to accept or reject certain beliefs which were previously foundational supports in your understanding of the baptism of the Holy Spirit and speaking in tongues, be bold, trust God, and do as the Scriptures admonishes us: "test all things" [I Thessalonians 5:21]. Led by inspiration of the Holy Spirit, the apostle Paul wrote that every prophesy and teaching must be tested— and agree with God's holy Word. We are admonished by the Lord Jesus himself to "love the Lord your God with all of your heart and with all of your soul, and with all of your mind" [Matthew 22:37] and to "seek first his kingdom and righteousness…" [Matthew 6:33].

Thus, we can rest in the facts that God loves us and his Word is true, unchanging, and liberating. If we are to continue growing in his grace and love, we must submit to him—surrendering our minds to his truth, which brings peace, and our hearts to his love, which brings joy. We must give the Lord the key to every door that we have either opened or closed on these topics so that his Spirit and his truth will be our guides through the maze of teachings, beliefs, and activities associated with the Spirit's baptism and tongues.

Chapter One

The Baptism of the Holy Spirit:
Mandatory for All Christians?

In this chapter, we will begin to explore and explain the foundational topic of the baptism of the Holy Spirit. Answers to common questions, such as those below, will be provided by God's Word to clearly and contextually explain this confusing supernatural experience.

- What is this baptism?
- Who gets to experience it?
- Why is it necessary?
- When does this spiritual phenomenon occur?
- How can I know if I've received this heavenly baptism by the Spirit?

The desired outcome of this book is the replacement of confusion about this topic with Scriptural clarity, contentment, and confidence in your salvation, sanctification, and power for serving the Lord.

In the verses below, Paul refers to the human body and its various parts as a physical illustration of what God is doing in the spiritual realm—building and equipping the "body of Christ" (the church = born-again believers) for his eternal purposes and glory.

> The body is a unit, though it is made up of many parts; and
> though all its parts are many, they form one body. So it is
> with Christ. For we were *all baptized by one Spirit into one*
> *body*—whether Jews or Greeks, slave or free—*and we were all*
> *given the one Spirit to drink.* [I Corinthians 12:12-13, emphasis
> added]

He reaffirms the spiritual truth that all believers are spiritually reborn
(born-again) only when, by the baptizing work of the Holy Spirit,
they are united with Christ in his death, burial, and resurrection. This
happens instantaneously when they act on Romans 10:9-13:

> That if you confess with your mouth, "Jesus is Lord," and
> believe in your heart that God raised him from the dead,
> you will be saved. For it is with your heart that you believe
> and are justified, and it is with your mouth that you confess
> and are saved. As the Scripture says, "Anyone who trusts in
> him will never be put to shame. For there is no difference
> between Jew and Gentile—the same Lord is Lord of all and
> richly blesses all who call on him, for, "Everyone who calls
> on the name of the Lord will be saved."

The only "work" that God requires of people in the process of being
spiritually regenerated (saved/spiritually born-again) is to place their
faith in Christ, confessing (agreeing) with God that they are sinners
and in need of forgiveness through the shed blood of Christ Jesus:

Then they asked him, "What must we do to do the works God requires?" Jesus answered, "The work of God is this: to believe in the one he has sent." [John 6:28-29]

Similarly, just as humans have a work to do in the process of salvation (to believe), God himself, by his Spirit, has a work to do in the spiritual realm to give every believer new birth and equip them with at least one spiritual gift.

Or don't you know that *all of us who were baptized* into Christ Jesus *were baptized into his death?* We were therefore *buried with him through baptism into death* in order that, just as Christ was *raised from the dead* through the glory of the Father, we too may live a new life. If we have been *united with him like this in his death,* we will certainly also be united with him in his resurrection. For we know that *our old self was crucified* with him *so that the body of sin might be done away with,* that we should *no longer be slaves to sin*— because *anyone who has died has been freed from sin.* [Romans 6:3-7]

From the previous verses, it is clear that physical baptism by water symbolizes being buried by the Holy Spirit into the death of Christ and raised/united with him in his resurrected life. This is the biblical baptism of the Holy Spirit. Scripturally, and thus factually, it is impossible for anyone to be born-again unless they experience the baptism of the Holy Spirit.

3

We must remember that the salvation of a soul, originally condemned by the law due to transgressions of God's commands, is accomplished by God in an uncompromised judicial manner. Romans 7 explains what occurs in a person's spiritual life judicially and legally, in God's "courtroom," when baptized into the death of Jesus.

Dead to Sin, Alive in Christ

> Do you not know, brothers and sisters—for I am speaking to those who know the law—that the law has authority over someone only as long as that person lives? For example, by law a married woman is bound to her husband as long as he is alive, but if her husband dies, she is released from the law that binds her to him. So then, if she has sexual relations with another man while her husband is still alive, she is called an adulteress. But if her husband dies, she is released from that law and is not an adulteress if she marries another man. So, my brothers and sisters, you also died to the law through the body of Christ, that you might belong to another, to him who was raised from the dead, in order that we might bear fruit for God. For when we were in the realm of the flesh, the sinful passions aroused by the law were at work in us, so that we bore fruit for death. [Romans 7:1-5]

Every person born after Adam was born with a sinful nature, inherited from Adam and Eve. The law of God indicates that all lawbreakers must be penalized (separated from him because he is holy and sin cannot be in his presence). When Adam and Eve disobeyed God, they became guilty as lawbreakers and classified as sinners. As their offspring, we inherited their corrupted spiritual DNA and, thus, were born with a sinful nature.

All people who have not trusted Christ as Savior have only one option for attempting to stand before God as justified and holy — upholding his law with perfection. Free of sin, a person can stand before God on their own merit as holy and acceptable. Without sinless perfection, however, they are in trouble. Trying but failing to perfectly keep God's law, or merely highly respecting his law, is not sufficient for being declared holy. The law cannot atone for our sin. It can only point out that we are guilty as lawbreakers and, therefore, are guilty and deserving of punishment. The law is not evil; it just cannot save us. Christ Jesus could pay the sin debt of all people because he lived a perfect life and fulfilled the law of God completely—without sin. When a person chooses to place their faith in Jesus Christ for salvation from the penalty of sin, they are baptized (united) into Christ's death by the Holy Spirit (see I Corinthians 12:13) and thus considered by God to be dead to God's law and released from the associated penalty.

As we know, baptism is not just about one being immersed/buried someone (symbolizing death); it's also about being raised to newness of life. When a person trusts Christ as Savior, God gives them new life (spiritual rebirth) and yokes them to Jesus. They are instantly credited with his righteousness and holiness by grace (free). They don't have to try fulfilling the law to be accepted by God as righteous in his sight. They have it by grace, married/yoked to the Holy One, Jesus.

> But now, by dying to what once bound us, we have been released from the law so that we serve in the new way of the Spirit, and not in the old way of the written code. [Romans 7:6]

The verse above meshes perfectly with our reading earlier regarding the necessary purpose of the baptism of the Holy Spirit (see Romans 6:1-10)—a baptism not by man into water but by God's Spirit into Christ's death. So, from both judicial and legal perspectives, God frees born-again believers (forever) from the penalty of eternal damnation for breaking his Laws. When they trust Christ Jesus as Savior and Lord, they are united with him in his death to the law by Holy Spirit baptism and raised to life, free from the condemnation of the law as new creatures in Christ. Legally and judicially before the Judge of the Universe, they are declared innocent, guiltless, and holy in Jesus.

In legal systems, "double jeopardy" is a defense procedure that prevents an accused person from being tried again on the same charges following an acquittal in the same jurisdiction. Since Jesus' death was sufficient to pay the penalty for all our sins, the person(s) baptized into his death and raised spiritually as a new creation free from the penalty of the law cannot, therefore, ever be tried by God's law for sin ever again. They have been pardoned, once for all time, for being a sinner. They are now associated wholly with Jesus' resurrection, righteousness, and holiness. Romans 7:6 concludes the free state of a Christian: "But now, by dying to what once bound us (the old husband, called the law), we have been released from the law (meaning the penalty/condemnation) so that we may serve in the new way of the Spirit, and not in the old way of the written code." This miraculous event that translates a person from being spiritually dead to becoming alive in Christ forevermore occurs by way of the baptism of the Holy Spirit.

Baptized, Circumcised, Naturalized

> In him you were also circumcised, in the putting off of the
> sinful nature, not with a circumcision done by the hands of
> men but with the circumcision done by Christ...
> [Colossians 2:11]

During the process of the mandatory spiritual baptism, one of the Spirit's vital actions is to circumcise the heart of the believer, who is being instantaneously translated from the kingdom of darkness (unrighteousness) to the kingdom of light (righteousness). Paul speaks about this spiritual circumcision in Romans 2:17-29, as he communicates truths regarding Jews and the Law. For the purpose of our study, we will review Romans 2:25-29 and 3:20 (emphasis added):

> Circumcision has value if you observe the law, but if you
> break the law, you have become as though you had not been
> circumcised. So then, if those who are not circumcised keep
> the law's requirements, will they not be regarded as though
> they were circumcised? The one who is not circumcised
> physically and yet obeys the law will condemn you who,
> even though you have the written code and circumcision,
> are a lawbreaker. A person is not a Jew who is one only
> outwardly, nor is circumcision merely outward and physical.
> No, a person is a Jew who is one inwardly; *and circumcision is
> circumcision of the heart, by the Spirit, not by the written code.* Such
> a person's praise is not from other people, but from God...
> Therefore no one will be declared righteous in God's sight
> by the works of the law; rather, through the law we become
> conscious of our sin.

Physical circumcision was vital in the sanctification of Israel from other nations. It was an outward operation done on the male body as an act of obedience to God, done by human hands as a foreshadowing of what the Holy Spirit would do in the hearts of people after Jesus' death, resurrection, and glorification back in heaven. God instituted this physical practice with Abraham, the father of God's chosen people [Genesis 17:11-14]:

> "You are to undergo circumcision, and it will be the sign of

the covenant between me and you. For the generations to come every male among you who is eight days old must be circumcised, including those born in your household or bought with money from a foreigner—those who are not your offspring. Whether born in your household or bought with your money, they must be circumcised. My covenant in your flesh is to be an everlasting covenant. Any uncircumcised male, who has not been circumcised in the flesh, will be cut off from his people; he has broken my covenant."

It was required that every male Jewish boy, on the eighth day of his life, have the flesh of his foreskin cut as a sign of the Abrahamic covenant. This command was solidified in the Mosaic Law as a lasting ordinance for the Jewish people:

On the eighth day the flesh of his foreskin shall be circumcised. [Leviticus 12:3]

This outward, physical practice was intended to be a picture of what the Spirit of God would do inwardly in believers. To be born-again, one's inner/real self (heart, mind, and soul) must first be cut by the Word of God. Just as a skilled surgeon uses cutting instruments such as scalpels and saws to cut/repair various parts of the body to bring about newness and restoration, God does this in the spiritual realm by way of his Spirit and Word:

Take the helmet of salvation and the sword of the Spirit, which is the word of God. [Ephesians 6:17]

For the word of God is alive and active. Sharper than any double-edged sword, it penetrates even to dividing soul and spirit, joints and marrow; it judges the thoughts and attitudes of the heart. [Hebrews 4:12]

Legal Indebtedness—Cancelled

The predicament of every soul who has not trusted in Jesus as their personal Savior is like that of a convicted felon waiting for the final judgment from the courts. They have been proven to be lawbreakers, and the judge will render a verdict that is consistent with what the law demands. Similarly, as the Bible indicates and our own lives validate, we are all born sinners and have transgressed God's laws. Thus, without the forgiveness of God, the penalty of transgressing his laws is eternal incarceration in the spiritual world's penitentiary—hell.

The only way that convicted criminals can escape the penalties of their crimes is if the court has mercy and shows leniency. A pardon is a governmental decision to allow a person to be relieved of some or all of the legal consequences resulting from a criminal conviction. A pardon may be granted before or after conviction for the crime, depending on the laws of the jurisdiction. In the United States of America, a state governor can offer a simple pardon, in which official forgiveness is granted for a crime for which a person has been convicted. Article II, Section 2 of the U.S. Constitution designates the president as the only person with the power to grant pardons and reprieves for federal crimes.

When considering the spiritual pardon that God offers sinners, it is vital to understand that the sinner's prayer, asking for forgiveness of sins, is not merely about speaking words emanating from a heart's conviction of sin. No, true spiritual conversion occurs when the sinner realizes the grave danger they are in as convicted lawbreakers before God's holy throne—and falls on the mercy of God through the shed blood of Jesus, thanking him for his loving mercy, grace, and willingness to forgive. Without receiving a pardon from God— who is the President of all presidents, Governor of all governors, and Warden of all wardens—the transgressor is on the road to an eternal sentence in hell. Without this understanding of the supreme urgency to repent and ask God for a pardon, the sinner's prayer will most likely lead to a failed attempt at trying to live the Christian life versus being born-again.

When a person sincerely calls on the name of the Lord in repentance to be saved from the penalty of sin, they are, in the spiritual realm, baptized into the death of Jesus and raised a new creation—forgiven of sin and adopted into the family of God. They are circumcised in the heart by the Holy Spirit, having their previously callous/hard/dead heart cut away and given a soft/living heart alive for God. This person is reborn spiritually—saved for eternity and set apart to God. It is a picture of the new birth, a picture of conversion.

> I will give you a new heart and put a new spirit in you; I will remove from you your heart of stone and give you a hear of flesh. [Ezekiel 36:26]

Hammering home this theological truth, which he stated in his letters to the Romans and Corinthians, the apostle Paul conveyed to the believers living in Colossae what the Holy Spirit does in the spiritual realm when people turn to God in repentance, confess their sin and need for forgiveness, and surrender to Christ as their Savior and Lord (emphasis added):

> *Having been buried with him in baptism,* in which you were also raised with him through your faith in the working of God, who raised him from the dead. *When you were dead in your sins and in the uncircumcision of your flesh, God made you alive with Christ. He forgave us all our sins, having canceled the charge of our legal indebtedness, which stood against us and condemned us; he has taken it away, nailing it to the cross.* And having disarmed the powers and authorities, he made a public spectacle of them, triumphing over them by the cross. [Colossians 2:12-15]

Reiterating what has been clearly established from previous Scripture references examined so far, the baptism that is referred to in the preceding verses is one done in the spiritual realm, by the third person of the Holy Trinity, to every repentant sinner who confesses Christ as their Savior. They are immersed/covered/baptized into the substitutionary death of Christ and are legally deemed dead to the Law. Raised by the Spirit from this baptism into newness of life—the resurrected life of Christ—the believer is thus spiritually born-again, free from the penalty of God's law—because the law has no power over one who has died.

> Since, then, you have been raised with Christ, set your hearts on things above, where Christ is, seated at the right hand of God. Set your minds on things above, not on earthly things. For you died, and your life is now hidden with Christ in God. [Colossians 3:1-3]

This spiritual baptism regenerates the spiritually dead dimension of humans who have three parts—spirit, soul, and body—into the death and resurrection of Christ Jesus. This is the biblical baptism of the Holy Spirit that happens at conversion. It is not a second blessing that happens subsequent to salvation. All people who confess their sins to God and call on the Lord Jesus Christ to save them experience this baptism. Without the baptism of the Holy Spirit, there is no salvation.

Next, we'll take a deep dive into the spiritual gift of tongues. Continue to allow the Word of God, line upon line, to guide your thinking and beliefs.

Chapter Two

Apostleship, Tongues, and the Great Commission

In Mark 6:30, Jesus' disciples are gathered around him, reporting about all that they had done and taught in his name. These twelve men, referred to as "the Twelve," were hand-picked by the Lord Jesus during his earthly ministry to be his apostles after his resurrection and ascension. The word apostle refers to one who is chosen and sent—with a special commission—as a directly appointed and fully authorized representative of the sender. In Hebrews 3:1, Jesus himself is referred to as the "apostle and high priest whom we confess," for he repeatedly spoke of himself as having been appointed and sent into the world by the Father. He stated over and over that he was appointed and sent by God the Father to be the Savior of all mankind:

> Anyone who welcomes you welcomes me, and anyone who welcomes me welcomes the one who sent me. [Matthew 10:40]

> He answered, "I was sent only to the lost sheep of Israel." [Matthew 15:24]

> Whoever welcomes one of these little children in my name

welcomes me; and whoever welcomes me does not welcome me but the one who sent me. [Mark 9:37]

The title "apostle" established the Twelve's authority as Christ's specially appointed envoys—men directly chosen by him and called to share the foundational truth of the gospel on which his church, the corporate body of all believers, would be built. Jesus commissioned these twelve men as his special delegates among the early disciples to be uniquely empowered by the Holy Spirit to convincingly accomplish his purposes.

I Corinthians is the New Testament letter written by Paul that not only contains teachings about spiritual gifts, including speaking (and interpreting) in tongues but also elaborates on the authenticity of his apostleship—which was being questioned by some and denied by others. Thus, as the topics of the baptism of the Holy Spirit and tongues are examined, it is highly important that readers of I Corinthians grasp the context and purpose behind the title apostle. The Great Commission, given by Jesus to the Twelve (minus one— Judas Iscariot, who betrayed Jesus and later committed suicide) and all subsequent believers, is recorded in the following verses and informs Christ's followers of (1) *his* authority and (2) *their* task:

All authority in heaven and on earth has been given to me. Therefore go and make disciples of all nations, baptizing them in the name of the Father and of the Son and of the Holy Spirit, and teaching them to obey all that I have commanded you. And surely I am with you always, to the very end of the age. [Matthew 28:18-20]

Acts 1:4-8 record the words Jesus spoke once again to the disciples, just before he ascended into heaven, reminding them of their call to help fulfill the Great Commission given by him:

> On one occasion, while he was eating with them, he gave them this command: "Do not leave Jerusalem, but wait for the gift my Father promised, which you have heard me speak about. For John baptized with water, but in a few days you will be baptized with the Holy Spirit." So when they met together, they asked him, "Lord, are you at this time going to restore the kingdom of Israel?" He said to them: "It is not for you to know the times or dates the Father has set by his own authority. But you will receive power when the Holy Spirit comes on you; and you will be my witnesses in Jerusalem, and in all Judea and Samaria, and to the ends of the earth."

The birth and early history of the church is recorded in Acts 1-10. It began with the apostles' evangelistic campaigns—first to the Jewish people, next to the Samaritans, and finally to the Gentiles—consistent with Jesus' words to them in Acts 1:8:

> But you will receive power when the Holy Spirit comes on you; and you will be my witnesses in Jerusalem, and in all

Judea and Samaria, and to the ends of the earth.

During this foundational period of the building of the church, when the door of heaven was first opened for sinners to enter by faith in Jesus, Peter was called by God to carry out a unique assignment purposed only for him. Jesus spoke of this in his prophetic words found in Matthew 16:19:

> I will give you the keys of the kingdom of heaven; whatever you bind on earth will be bound in heaven, and whatever you loose on earth will be loosed in heaven.

Jesus was signifying by the words above that prior to his resurrection and being exalted back to the right hand of the throne of God the Father, heaven's "door" had been closed to all people—sinners. Peter would be given the "keys" of the kingdom by Jesus to open (unlock) the door to heaven by preaching the Good News of Jesus so that, by placing their faith in him, people of every walk of life could hear the message of salvation, receive forgiveness of sins, and enter into an everlasting relationship with God.

The Jewish people, to whom the Messiah (Christ) was biologically linked in his humanity, saw all people in the world as belonging to one of three camps: Jews (including non-Jews who converted to Judaism), Samaritans (half-Jewish), and Gentiles (non-Jewish). The spiritual keychain given to Peter by Jesus had three different keys: one for each of the aforementioned groups. We see in the first ten

18

chapters of Acts how Peter used these "keys of the kingdom" [Matthew 16:19] with apostolic authority and power to open the doors of faith to each of these groups:

- Jews [Acts 2]
- Samaritans [Acts 8]
- Gentiles [Acts 10]

Thus, the fulfillment of the Great Commission had begun. In subsequent chapters, we will take a closer look at how each of the three people groups listed above was initially given access to the door of heaven, which had been unlocked and opened for entry after Pentecost. The goal is to understand the necessity of the baptism of the Holy Spirit and the purpose of tongues. The next chapter will offer greater insight into God's (1) invitation to all for entrance into his kingdom on equal footing, (2) desire to fill every disciple with his Spirit for holy living, and (3) empowerment of his disciples for effective ministry to win the lost.

Chapter Three

God's Kingdom and Christ's Body:
Jewish Inclusion

Examining God's intentions, plans, and actions on the day of Pentecost [Acts 2:1-41], after Christ's resurrection and ascension into heaven, is an absolute necessity in the quest to understand the baptism of the Holy Spirit and its link to the spiritual gift of speaking in tongues. Therefore, we must comb through the book of Acts to review the foundational truths regarding God's eternal purpose in Christ Jesus: redeeming souls and building the diverse and globally represented body of Christ—the church.

For the first seven chapters of the book of Acts, Jesus' church, the sum total of all who had trusted him as Savior and were born-again, consisted only of Jews—people who were biologically Jewish and those who converted to Judaism. This collective core group of Jews included the following people:

- The 120 people who were the first recipients of the Holy Spirit [Acts 1:15; 2:1-4]

- The 3,000+ that Peter spoke to at Pentecost [Acts 2:4-41]

- Nicolas, one of the first seven deacons who was a proselyte, a Gentile who had previously converted to Judaism [Acts 6:5]

On the day of Pentecost, with the 120 assembled, God clearly provided spectacular signs to Jews and proselytes from "every nation under heaven" [Acts 2:5] to indicate that the Holy Spirit had entered the earthly realm from heaven to spiritually convert, indwell, and fill/empower the first of many believers in Jesus.

With the goal of learning biblical truths about the baptism of the Holy Spirit and speaking in tongues, it is important to understand why God commanded the Jewish people to celebrate certain feasts (or festivals). Two in particular are Passover and Pentecost.

> ***Passover*** is the Jewish holiday that commemorates the Israelites' liberation by **God** from slavery in **Egypt** and their freedom as a nation under the leadership of **Moses**. It occurs fifty days before Pentecost. In the book of Exodus, which chronicles the ten plagues that God brought upon Egypt to cause Pharaoh to release the Israelite (Hebrew) slaves, the tenth plague was the death of all the firstborn in Egypt. God instructed the Jews to mark the doorposts of their **homes** with the blood of a slain lamb so that the Spirit of the Lord knew to *pass over* their homes rather than kill their firstborn. Hence, the English name Passover (from the Hebrew word *Pesakh*) for this holiday. Because God instructed the Jews not to eat any leavened bread during Passover, it is also called the Feast of Unleavened Bread. Read Exodus 12 to learn

more about God's purposes and instructions for Passover.

Pentecost comes from the Greek word *Pentēkostē*, which means "fiftieth." The word is derived from the Hebrew word *Shavuot*, known as the Feast of Harvest (or the Festival of Weeks), and refers to the festival celebrated on the fiftieth day (seven weeks and one day) after Passover.

The religious practices of the Jews during Passover and Pentecost were merely foreshadowing God's holy sacrificial and worship requirements, ultimately fulfilled by Jesus, the Lamb of God. The true Passover, for all who place their faith in Jesus, was fulfilled by Jesus' death on the cross, with his blood being poured out for the sins of the world. All who believe in him have their sins forgiven, and God's judgment, which would bring eternal damnation to them because of their sin, is placed on Jesus—the Lamb of God sacrificed as the sin-bearer for the world. Therefore, all who place their faith in him have the judgment of God *pass over* them. They are granted forgiveness of sin, the promise of eternal life, and future rewards as heirs of God's inheritance.

Fifty days was the time span from Christ's crucifixion (fulfilling his role as the Passover Lamb) to Pentecost. These fifty days included his resurrection, appearance to his disciples for forty days [Acts 1:3], and the few days that spanned from his ascension back into heaven

[Acts 1:8-11] until the day of Pentecost [Acts 2:1]. On the day of Pentecost, there were three main signs that God supernaturally performed to indicate that the Holy Spirit had been sent by Jesus into the world: (1) an audible sound like a violent wind came from heaven, (2) visible tongues of fire appeared in the air and came to rest on the 120, and (3) the 120 supernaturally spoke in the native languages of people from fourteen countries represented at Pentecost that day:

> Now there were staying in Jerusalem God-fearing Jews from every nation under heaven. When they heard this sound, a crowd came together in bewilderment, because each one heard their own language being spoken. Utterly amazed, they asked: "Aren't all these who are speaking Galileans? Then how is it that each of us hears them in our native language? Parthians, Medes and Elamites; residents of Mesopotamia, Judea and Cappadocia, Pontus and Asia, Phrygia and Pamphylia, Egypt and the parts of Libya near Cyrene; visitors from Rome (both Jews and converts to Judaism); Cretans and Arabs—we hear them declaring the wonders of God in our own tongues!" [Acts 2:5-11]

We see in the verses above that God used the three aforementioned supernatural signs to do what all signs are created to do: direct people in the proper way (protocol) to the desired destination (end goal). Jesus is the Way; heaven is the destination. Acts 2:12 tells us the following about the thousands who saw and heard the miraculous signs:

> Amazed and perplexed, they asked one another, "What
> does this mean?"

As relayed to us in Acts 2:14-41, Peter answered the people's question, explaining the meaning of the miracle they had just encountered: hearing 120 Jews speak in languages they had not previously known. Peter shared God's eternal plan to redeem mankind by way of the sacrificial death of the Messiah, the Lord Jesus Christ. Acts 2:41 tells us:

> Those who accepted his message were baptized, and about
> three thousand were added to their number that day.

The authenticity of the Holy Spirit's entry into the world as the One who would come to indwell believing Jews was undeniably and supernaturally verified to the thousands of eyewitnesses present at Pentecost after Jesus' death, burial, and resurrection. Thus, the sign of tongues fulfilled its purpose: moving unbelievers to marvel at God's power for the purpose of preparing them to hear the Good News of Jesus. Immediately after the Jews at Pentecost heard and saw the miracle of tongues, Peter was provided the platform to preach the gospel. This, in turn, allowed the Holy Spirit to fulfill his purpose for coming into the world: to convict the world of sin, righteousness, and judgment [John 16:7-11]. What was the result of the sign gifts at Pentecost plus the preaching of the gospel by Peter plus the convicting power of the Holy Spirit? Over 3,000 Jewish men surrendered to the lordship of Jesus Christ—and this does not include any women or youth in attendance. Wow! With this event, Peter began to fulfill Jesus' prophetic command given to him in Matthew 16:19, using the keys of the kingdom of heaven—preaching the Good News of Jesus with the authority given to him by God—to "open the door" of heaven. First, for the Jews. We will see that by the leading and confirmation of the Holy Spirit, Peter did the same for both the Samaritans and Gentiles, fulfilling God's plan for him to use the keys of the kingdom to open the door of salvation to all three people groups on earth.

Chapter Four

God's Kingdom and Christ's Body:
Samaritan Inclusion

Before Jesus ascended back into heaven after his resurrection, he spent forty days on earth speaking to the eleven apostles and other disciples about the kingdom of God. He told them to wait for the promised Holy Spirit [Luke 24:49; Acts 1:4-8; Acts 2:33] and then, afterward, to go throughout Jerusalem, Judea and Samaria, and to the ends of the earth as his witnesses:

> Then Jesus came to them and said, "All authority in heaven and on earth has been given to me. Therefore go and make disciples of all nations, baptizing them in the name of the Father and of the Son and of the Holy Spirit, and teaching them to obey everything I have commanded you. And surely I am with you always, to the very end of the age." [Matthew 28:18-20]

The Lord's commandment to his eleven apostles and early disciples was to share the truth of God with all people, imploring them to repent, trust Jesus as Savior, and walk in willful obedience to his lordship. His command was not only specific regarding the content of their message but also crystal clear on where (and with whom) to share it. His apostles and first disciples, however—all Jews (including Jewish proselytes)—did not yet grasp that God's plan of salvation was inclusive of all people. They had not yet comprehended that non-Jews would also be redeemed as co-heirs with Jews. Thus, they had no intention of going to the Samaritans and Gentiles. Because of their unique and historical relationship with God and their cultural, religious, and racial biases, their hearts and minds were still closed to the belief that non-Jews would share in the inheritance of God's kingdom with them.

The truth is that they did not attempt to fulfill the Great Commission beyond Jerusalem and to non-Jews until after the church in Jerusalem began to experience persecution, as recorded in Acts 7:54–8:3. The Bible tells us what happened to the church on the day that Stephen, one of the first seven deacons of the church, was stoned to death:

> On that day a great persecution broke out against the church at Jerusalem, and all except the apostles were scattered throughout Judea and Samaria. Godly men buried Stephen and mourned deeply for him. But Saul began to destroy the church. Going from house to house, he dragged off men and women and put them in prison. [Acts 8:1(b)-3]

In Acts 8:12, Philip (one of the seven original deacons), after being forced out of Jerusalem because of the persecution, found himself finally doing what Jesus commanded his followers to do in the Great Commission [Matthew 28:18-20]—he preached the Good News of Jesus to Samaritans and baptized them in the name of Jesus:

When the apostles in Jerusalem heard that Samaria had accepted the word of God, they sent Peter and John to them. When they arrived, they prayed for them that they might receive the Holy Spirit, because the Holy Spirit had not yet come upon any of them; they had simply been baptized into the name of the Lord Jesus. Then Peter and John placed their hands on them, and they received the Holy Spirit [Acts 8:14-17].

***

Now for a Brief Q&A Session

Question: What did Peter and John do when they saw that the Samaritans trusted Jesus?

Answer: They openly and publicly laid their hands on them.

Question: What happened when the apostles laid their hands on the Samaritans?

Answer: The Holy Spirit came upon them—in the same way that he came upon the eleven apostles and the other 109 people with them (all Jews) as recorded in Acts 2:1-21.

Question: Why was it necessary for the two apostles to come and lay hands on the Samaritans?

Answer: To openly prove to all people that God was accepting the

Samaritans who trusted Christ Jesus as Savior—in the same way that he accepted the Jewish believers. Remember, too, that it was Peter, not Philip, who Jesus said would be given the keys with which to open the door for the entry of the three people-groups into heaven [Matthew 16:19]. As an authoritative apostle of Jesus, Peter's endorsement, through his word and physical touch, validated the Samaritans' acceptance by God and inclusion in the body of Christ.

***

During Jesus' three-year earthly ministry, an incident involving him and a Samaritan exposed the animosity between Jews and Samaritans. Interactions between the two people groups were frowned upon, and a Jewish person would never consider openly touching or embracing (emotionally and physically) a Samaritan. This act would be, simply stated, unthinkable. In John 4:9, we see that a Jew became ceremonially unclean (man-made religious laws) if he used a drinking cup handled by a Samaritan:

> The Samaritan woman said to him, "You are a Jew and I am a Samaritan woman. How can you ask me for a drink?" (For Jews do not associate with Samaritans.)

Besides theological differences, racial bias had also crept into Jewish thought, convincing Jews that they were superior to the Samaritans and that God would only accept Jews as inheritors of his glorious kingdom. God's plan, however, was not only to reconcile both people groups to himself but also to reconcile them with each other.

Another Scriptural example of the relational discord between Jews and Samaritans—and the overriding love of God in Christ that would soon bring them together—is illuminated in Jesus' story of the Good Samaritan, found in Luke 10:25-37:

> On one occasion an expert in the law stood up to test Jesus. "Teacher," he asked, "what must I do to inherit eternal life?"
>
> "What is written in the Law?" he replied. "How do you read it?"
>
> He answered, "'Love the Lord your God with all your heart and with all your soul and with all your strength and with all your mind; and, 'Love your neighbor as yourself.'"
>
> "You have answered correctly," Jesus replied. "Do this and you will live."
>
> But he wanted to justify himself, so he asked Jesus, "And who is my neighbor?"
>
> In reply Jesus said: "A man was going down from Jerusalem to Jericho, when he was attacked by robbers. They stripped him of his clothes, beat him and went away, leaving him half dead. A priest happened to be going down the same road,

and when he saw the man, he passed by on the other side. So too, a Levite, when he came to the place and saw him, passed by on the other side. But a Samaritan, as he traveled, came where the man was; and when he saw him, he took pity on him. He went to him and bandaged his wounds, pouring on oil and wine. Then he put the man on his own donkey, brought him to an inn and took care of him. The next day he took out two denarii and gave them to the innkeeper. 'Look after him,' he said, 'and when I return, I will reimburse you for any extra expense you may have.' Which of these three do you think was a neighbor to the man who fell into the hands of robbers?"

The expert in the law replied, "The one who had mercy on him." Jesus told him, "Go and do likewise."

Samaritans – A Brief History

The Samaritans were a people of mixed heritage that came about after Assyria conquered Israel [II Kings 17:24-41] about 700 years before the birth of Christ. The backdrop to this story is that the kingdom of Israel had been split into two sections: the Northern Kingdom (comprised of ten of the twelve tribes), which retained the name Israel, and the Southern Kingdom (comprised of two of the twelve tribes, Judah and Benjamin), which was called Judah. After the separation of Judah and Israel in the ninth century, King Omri of the Northern Kingdom bought the hill of Samaria from a man named

Shemer, from which the name Samaria is derived [1 Kings 16:24]. He built the city of Samaria there, which became the capital of the Northern Kingdom of Israel.

Assyrian King Tiglath-Pileser began plundering Israel (the ten northern tribes) in 740 BC [II Kings 15:29]. In 722 BC, Samaria was finally taken by the Assyrians under the rule of Sargon II. While many of the Israelite inhabitants of the city and the surrounding area of Samaria were led off into captivity, some farmers and others (poor) were left behind. The Assyrians then imported **Gentiles into Samaria**. The remaining Israelites intermarried with the new Gentile settlers, and the resulting **mixed-heritage people group came to be known as the Samaritans.**

In the story of the Good Samaritan [Luke 10:25-37], Jesus commended the one in the story that the Jewish people thought of least and even rejected: the Samaritan. The Jews despised the Samaritans and considered them "half-breeds" physically. Jesus knew all of this, and that's why initially, while on earth for three years laying the foundation of the gospel of grace, he did not have the twelve disciples go to other people groups—the Samaritans and Gentiles:

> These twelve Jesus sent out with the following instructions: "Do not go among the Gentiles or enter any town of the Samaritans. Go rather to the lost sheep of Israel. As you go, proclaim this message: 'The kingdom of heaven has come

near.' Heal the sick, raise the dead, cleanse those who have leprosy, drive out demons. Freely you have received; freely give." [Matthew 10:5-8]

Desegregation: Jews and Samaritans

Going back to the scene of Acts 8:14-17, it is now quite clear how monumental it was for Peter and John to physically lay hands on the Samaritans who had received Jesus as Savior and Lord—physically, emotionally, and spiritually embracing/validating them as equal members in the family of God. The doubting Jewish believers were now convinced that the Samaritans equally received the gift of the Holy Spirit, drinking the same "spiritual drink" from the same proverbial cup as prophesied by Jesus:

> On the last and greatest day of the Feast, Jesus stood and said in a loud voice, 'If anyone is thirsty, let him come to me and drink. Whoever believes in me, as the Scripture has said, streams of living water will flow from within him.' By this he meant the Spirit, whom those who believed in him were later to receive. Up to that time the Spirit had not been given, since Jesus had not yet been glorified. [John 7:37-39]

When Peter and John were sent by the Jerusalem church to investigate the report that Samaritans were responding to the Gospel of Jesus, they may have begun to cautiously believe that God might indeed be allowing Samaritans to become members of his household of faith. This is because they had experienced a few isolated events during Jesus' earthly ministry wherein Samaritans submitted to Jesus as Messiah. One example is the Samaritan woman Jesus encountered at the well and the other Samaritans who placed their faith in Jesus as a result, as recorded in John 4:39-42:

> Many of the Samaritans from that town believed in him because of the woman's testimony, "He told me everything I ever did." So when the Samaritans came to him, they urged him to stay with them, and he stayed two days. And because of his words many more become believers. They said to the woman, "We no longer believe just because of what you said; now we have heard for ourselves, and we know that this man really is the Savior of the world."

This incident occurred before the resurrection of Jesus, however, and was not openly shared because they would have been severely criticized, even ostracized, by other Jews. So, en masse, the Jewish followers of Jesus had not even contemplated that Samaritans would be brought into the family of God through Jesus—even though he had given them the mandate to share the gospel with everyone after his ascension into heaven.

Consider the following scenario that confirms this fact and reveals the animosity that existed between Jews and Samaritans:

> As the time approached for him to be taken up to heaven,

Jesus resolutely set out for Jerusalem. And he sent messengers ahead, who went into a Samaritan village to get things ready for him; but the people there did not welcome him, because he was heading for Jerusalem. When the disciples James and John saw this, they asked, "Lord, do you want us to call fire down from heaven to destroy them?" But Jesus turned and rebuked them, and they went to another village. [Luke 9:51-56]

The pouring out of the Holy Spirit onto the Samaritans, with the same proof signs that accompanied the pouring out of the Spirit on the Jews at Pentecost, was God's verification to all that (1) the Samaritans were not spiritually "unclean" and (2) they would drink the same cup and be baptized with the same Spirit:

Then James and John, the sons of Zebedee, came to him. "Teacher," they said, "we want you to do for us whatever we ask." "What do you want me to do for you?" he asked. They replied, "Let one of us sit at your right and the other at your left in your glory." "You don't know what you are asking," Jesus said. "Can you drink the cup I drink or be baptized with the baptism I am baptized with?" "We can," they answered. Jesus said to them, "You will drink the cup I drink and be baptized with the baptism I am baptized with, but to sit at my right or left is not for me to grant. These places belong to those for whom they have been prepared."

[Mark 10:35-40]

The statement "to drink the cup that someone else drinks" means to share in the same experience or fate as someone else, whether by free will or by force. Thus, when the Holy Spirit came upon the Samaritans like he had come on Jesus and the Jews, with the same visible and audible signs from heaven, God validated his acceptance of them and verified that they, too, were consecrated, approved, and accepted by him.

If feelings of pride or superiority develop in some members of a group, feelings of resentment or unworthiness may crop up in the other segment(s) of that group. This is true for a business, sports team, family, and even the body of Christ. We see that this scenario began to play out in the early days of the church when it was comprised only of Jews. Acts 6:1-4 tell us:

> In those days when the number of disciples was increasing, the Grecian Jews among them complained against the Hebraic Jews because their widows were being overlooked in the daily distribution of food. So the Twelve gathered all the disciples together and said, "It would not be right for us to neglect the ministry of the word of God in order to wait on tables. Brothers, choose seven men from among you who are known to be full of the Spirit and wisdom. We will turn this responsibility over to them and will give our attention to prayer and the ministry of the word."

Rest assured, if drama like this occurred among those who had the same original religious foundation (Judaism)—who had come into the saving knowledge of Jesus but had unresolved racial/ethnic tension—then how much more would the mental and social barriers between the Jewish and Samaritan believers must be overcome for unity to be possible. God calls us to let go of all beliefs that don't align with Jesus alone as our salvation and sufficiency. In God's sight, there are no racial groups more superior than others. However, enmity in the body of Christ is what Satan desires:

> The acts of the flesh are obvious: sexual immorality, impurity and debauchery; idolatry and witchcraft; hatred, discord, jealousy, fits of rage, selfish ambition, dissensions, factions and envy; drunkenness, orgies, and the like. I warn you, as I did before, that those who live like this will not inherit the kingdom of God. [Galatians 5:19-21]

There is not one member of the body of Christ who is greater or more important than others:

> The body is a unit, though it is made up of many parts; and though its parts are many, they form one body. So it is with Christ. For we were all baptized by one Spirit into one body—whether Jews or Greeks, slave or free—and we were all given the one Spirit to drink. Now the body is not made up of one part but of many. [I Corinthians 12:12-14]

But God has combined the members of the body and has given greater honor to the parts that lacked it, so that there should be no division in the body, but that its parts should have equal concern for each other. [I Corinthians 12:24(b)-25]

In summary, God drove home the message of his acceptance of the Samaritans into the household of faith in the hearts and minds of both Jews and Samaritans. The validating proof-sign that God allowed to manifest after the Samaritans had accepted the gospel and Peter and John laid hands on them was speaking in tongues (known human languages), just as Peter and John had at Pentecost. It was now shockingly irrefutable in the minds of the Jewish believers that God accepted the Samaritans as equal members in the body of Christ (the church). His message was that they (Jewish believers) must now accept the Samaritan believers as equal members in the household of God. The Samaritans' speaking in tongues was not normative but highly mandatory at that critical juncture when God was laying the foundation of the church and opening the door of faith to the once-ostracized and rejected Samaritans.

Chapter Five

God's Kingdom and Christ's Body:
Gentile Inclusion

The Bible first refers to people as Gentiles (non-Jews) in a prophetic section of the Old Testament where God the Father is speaking about God the Son—and how he would send him into the world as a humble and suffering servant for the purpose of redeeming mankind:

> "I, the LORD, have called you in righteousness; I will take hold of your hand. I will keep you and make you to be a covenant for the people and a light for the Gentiles, to open eyes that are blind, to free captives from prison and to release from the dungeon those who sit in darkness." [Isaiah 42:6]

Note that God's words are crystal clear that the Messiah (Christ) would come to set not only Jews free from the power and penalty of sin but also Gentiles (non-Jews). During both Isaiah's time and Jesus' earthly ministry, the Jews did not believe that Gentiles would one day be accepted by the Messiah and be brought into the same state of acceptance by God as they were.

The next Old Testament reference to non-Jews as Gentiles is found in Isaiah 49:6:

> [He says]: "It is too small a thing for you to be my servant
> to restore the tribes of Jacob and bring back those of Israel
> I have kept. I will also make you a light for the Gentiles, that
> you may bring my salvation to the ends of the earth."

Fast-forwarding to the New Testament, the first mention of the word
Gentiles is found in Luke 2:32, and it references the prophecy of
Isaiah 42:6:

> Now there was a man in Jerusalem called Simeon, who was
> righteous and devout…Moved by the Spirit, he went into
> the temple courts. When the parents brought in the child
> Jesus to do for him what the custom of the law required,
> Simeon took him in his arms and praised God, saying:
>
> "Sovereign Lord, as you have promised, you now dismiss
> your servant in peace. For my eyes have seen your salvation,
> which you have prepared in the sight of all people, a light
> for revelation to the Gentiles and for glory to your people
> Israel." [Luke 2:25-32]

So it is evident that God clearly communicated to both the Jews and
the rest of the world that he would one day redeem Gentiles and Jews
on the same footing of faith. Both would become co-heirs of God's
kingdom. To the Jew, who was blinded to this truth, this thought was
unthinkable.

In both the Old and New Testaments, God pre-ordained that the first mention of the term Gentiles be used in a positive light to articulate with no question or ambiguity that his plan was to bring salvation to the Gentiles.

While the mind of God was quite clear regarding his eternal plans to redeem both Jew and Gentile, the mindset of Jews toward Gentiles was not consistent with God's. In the same way that there was enmity between Jews and Samaritans, so it was also between Jews and Gentiles. One factor that led Jews to not mingle with Gentiles was the strong influence of religious rituals and ceremonies that the Jews created, in addition to what God commanded. Over the years, in addition to the laws and commands God gave them (the Torah, the Hebrew Bible), Jewish elders and teachers of the law created many ceremonies and traditions that were strictly followed—often elevating them even over God's Word. These ceremonies and traditions of men were collected over the years in what is known as the Talmud, which is comprised of two components: the Mishnah (the original written version of Judaism's oral law) and the Gemara (the record of the rabbinic discussions/commentaries of the Mishnah). The Talmud contains their opinions and interpretations, many of which are not accurate with regard to biblical interpretation or application.

During his earthly ministry, Jesus addressed the Jewish leaders many times about their allegiance to man-made teachings and traditions rather than to God's commands. One example is found in the seventh chapter of Mark:

> (The Pharisees and all the Jews do not eat unless they give their hands a ceremonial washing, holding to the traditions of the elders. When they come from the marketplace they do not eat unless they wash. And they observe many other traditions, such as the washing of cups, pitchers and kettles.) So the Pharisees and teachers of the law asked Jesus, "Why don't your disciples live according to the tradition of the elders instead of eating food without 'unclean' hands?" [Mark 7:3-5]

Jesus' words of rebuke were aimed directly at their willful adherence to traditions of men (Talmud) rather than the holy Scriptures (Torah):

> He replied, "Isaiah was right when he prophesied about you hypocrites; as it is written: 'These people honor me with their lips, but their hearts are far from me. They worship me in vain; their teachings are but rules taught by men.' You have let go of the commands of God and are holding on to the traditions of men." And he said to them: "You have a fine way of setting aside the commands of God in order to observe your own traditions!" [Mark 7:6-9]

It is important to note that many of the ceremonies the Jews carried out had to do with their goal of becoming "clean" from associating with Gentiles. Jesus referred to the erroneous traditions and ceremonies as "yeast of the Pharisees," meaning teachings and practices that were not biblical and were spread to confuse and mislead others. These teachings and requirements infected the minds of all Jews—including Jesus' disciples. This included Peter, whom Jesus would use to unlock the door of faith to the Gentiles.

Peter was bound to two primary belief systems from which the Lord Jesus would have to liberate him: racial bias and religious error. The faulty teachings and traditions of men via the Talmud—to which he was culturally, mentally, and religiously bound—kept Gentiles ostracized from him. He deemed them to be unclean and inferior. Prior to being born-again and finally understanding the truth, his former religious conviction—Judaism (living by the law to be accepted by God)—prevented him from believing that striving to obey the laws and commands given to the Hebrews by God was not the pathway to eternal life. He was yoked to the belief that doing good works, living morally upright, and giving sacrificially (tithes and offerings) were the things he had to do to be accepted by God.

Like all other faithful followers of Judaism, he would also earnestly attempt to bind others to this religious way of life, a works-based theology. Jesus was going to free him from the binding chains of religious and racial superiority—and then use him to unlock the door of forgiveness of sins and entry into the kingdom of heaven for Jews, Samaritans, and Gentiles:

45

I will give you the keys of the kingdom of heaven; whatever

you bind on earth will be bound in heaven, and whatever

you loose on earth will be loosed in heaven. [Matthew 16:19]

Acts 10:44 reveals that while Peter was preaching the Good News of the kingdom of God to Cornelius and other Gentiles, they surrendered to God's truth and the lordship of Jesus. They believed in their hearts and received the three gifts that all believers receive when they repent of their sins and turn to Jesus Christ as their Lord and Savior: (1) forgiveness of sins, (2) adoption into God's family as his children [John 1:12,13], and (3) the gift of the Holy Spirit, who comes to indwell all who submit to the rule of King Jesus. The purpose of the indwelling Spirit of God is to empower believers to (1) *be* who they are as new creations in Christ [II Corinthians 5:17] and his ambassadors in the world [II Corinthians 5:20] and (2) *do* what he commands them to do [Philippians 2:13].

Peter's Victory Over Racial and Religious Bias

As recorded in Acts 10:34-48, Peter finally came to understand that God accepted even Gentile believers in Christ Jesus - in the same way he accepted penitent Jewish believers. Peter's arrival to this place of spiritual understanding and eradicated racial bias—expressed in his open and loving acceptance of both Samaritans and Gentiles—was finally accomplished after three years of journeying with Jesus. At the conclusion of Acts 10, he completed the "key" assignment given to him by the Lord Jesus. Peter used the spiritual keys of the kingdom of God (the Word of God) to open the door of heaven (by faith in Jesus) to each people group: the Jews, the Samaritans, and the Gentiles. He untied himself from the spiritual bonds of racial and religious pride and loosened the hearers of the Word of God from the spiritual shackles in which Satan had kept them bound. Finally understanding Jesus' words and plan, he said the following:

> I now realize how true it is that God does not show favoritism but accepts from every nation the one who fears him and does what is right. [Acts 10:34-35]

When the Gentile believers received forgiveness of sins and became indwelt by the Holy Spirit in the same supernatural way as the new Jewish believers had in Acts 2, the Bible tells us that Peter's companions (Jewish men who had trusted Christ as Savior and Lord) had doubts about being with the Gentile heathen. They had great inner conflict and found it almost impossible to believe that Gentiles would be accepted by God and inherit his kingdom, too—until God confirmed his acceptance of non-Jews with the same outward manifestation of the Holy Spirit that had occurred with the apostles and the other Jews in Acts 2:1-4:

> While Peter was still speaking these words, the Holy Spirit came on all who heard the message. The circumcised believers who had come with Peter were astonished that the gift of the Holy Spirit had been poured out even on

Gentiles. For they heard them speaking in tongues and praising God. [Acts 10:44-46]

After seeing and hearing the Gentile believers enter the kingdom of God and be treated by God's Spirit in the same ways as the Jewish and Samaritan believers, validated by the outward sign of tongues, Peter joyfully and victoriously said:

> Surely no one can stand in the way of their being baptized with water. They have received the Holy Spirit just as we have. So he ordered that they be baptized in the name of Jesus Christ. Then they asked Peter to stay with them for a few days. [Acts 10:47-48]

Peter's Stance Against Racial Bias

Peter and the six Jewish men (new believers in Jesus) who had gone with him to Cornelius' house [Acts 10:23(b) and 11:12(b)] had seen and heard heavenly proofs that God was accepting all people under heaven who surrendered to the lordship of Jesus Christ. They finally embraced this truth. Sadly, however, Scripture reveals that many Jewish converts to Christianity, referred to also as circumcised believers, were having extreme difficulty accepting the notion that Gentile believers were on equal footing before God:

> The apostles and the believers throughout Judea heard that the Gentiles also had received the word of God. So when Peter went up to Jerusalem, the circumcised

believers criticized him and said, "You went into the house of uncircumcised men and ate with them." [Acts 11:1-3]

Rather than rejoicing with Peter over the fact that Gentiles were now entering the kingdom of God, they criticized Peter for going into the house of a Gentile. What was Peter's response? He unapologetically explained everything that happened regarding Cornelius and his household's redemption by God. He was quick to tell those criticizing him about his vision from God [Acts 10:9-16] in which he was commanded by the Lord to kill and eat animals considered in Judaism to be "impure" and "unclean." He told them this to convey that, prior to meeting Cornelius, he was still adhering to the traditions of the elders. However, he went on to tell them what happened when he entered Cornelius' house and began to share the truth of Jesus:

> As I began to speak, the Holy Spirit came on them as he had come on us at the beginning. Then I remembered what the Lord had said: "John baptized with water, but you will be baptized with the Holy Spirit." So if God gave them the same gift as he gave us, who believed in the Lord Jesus Christ, was I to think that I could oppose God? When they heard this, they had no further objections and praised God, saying, "So then, even to the Gentiles God has granted repentance that leads to life." [Acts 11:15-18]

Verse eighteen is important in two ways: (1) the Jewish Christians had no further objections and accepted the Gentiles as their new brothers, and (2) the Jewish Christians praised God for opening the door of faith to Gentiles!

Question: Did the Jewish Christians praise (glorify) God in Acts 11:18 because God gave the Gentiles the ability to speak in tongues (other languages as he allowed them to do at Pentecost)?

Answer: No. Their praises to God had nothing to do with the Gentiles speaking in tongues. Rather, their praises to God were because, as they stated, "God has granted even the Gentiles repentance unto life."

> Thanks be to God because, when given the gift of life, we have every spiritual blessing in Christ! [Ephesians 1:3]

Chapter Six

Paul's Heavenly Calling and Spiritual Gifts

A s previously defined, an apostle is one directly chosen and sent with a special commission by the sender—as their fully-authorized representative. In Acts 9:15, the Lord says to Ananias, "This man [Saul of Tarsus, whose name Jesus changed to Paul] is my chosen instrument to carry my name before the Gentiles and their kings and before the people of Israel." Examining what Jesus said to Ananias, we see that his words "is my chosen instrument" could be restated "is my apostle." Paul verified and defended his apostolic calling many times throughout his ministry:

> I want you to know, brothers, that the gospel I preached is not something that man made up. I did not receive it from any man, nor was I taught it; rather, I received it by revelation from Jesus Christ... But when God, who set me apart from birth and called me by his grace, was pleased to reveal his Son in me so that I might preach him among the Gentiles, I did not consult any man, nor did I go to Jerusalem to see those who were apostles before I was, but I went immediately into Arabia and later returned to Damascus. [Galatians 1:11-17]

> Fourteen years later I went up again to Jerusalem, this time

with Barnabas. I took Titus along also. I went in response to a revelation and set before them the gospel that I preach among the Gentiles... they saw that I had been entrusted with the task of preaching the gospel to the Gentiles just as Peter had been to the Jews. For God, who was at work in the ministry of Peter as an apostle to the Jews, was also at work in my ministry as an apostle to the Gentiles. [Galatians 2:1-8]. [I Timothy 2:7]

Tongues, A Sign to Prove Paul's Apostleship

Reviewing background information about Paul's apostleship is highly relevant in developing a coherent understanding of what Scripture reveals about the baptism of the Holy Spirit with the evidence of speaking in tongues. As discussed while reviewing Acts 2–5, Peter fulfilled his calling as the apostle that Jesus authorized to use the "keys of the kingdom" [Matthew 16:19] to open the door of faith to the Jews. In Acts 8:14-17, Peter also used the keys of the kingdom of God (the preaching of the Good News of Jesus) to open the door to the Samaritans, validating that the Samaritans received the gift of salvation and baptism of the Holy Spirit just as the Jewish believers had at Pentecost [Acts 2:1-4]. In Acts 10, Peter used the keys to open the door of faith and the gift of the Holy Spirit to the Gentiles.

Thus, in chapters 1–10 of the book of Acts, we see that Peter opened the door of faith to all three people groups, with God himself validating his equal acceptance of them all by the miraculous signs that marked their spiritual baptism by the Holy Spirit. Notice that Peter's apostleship was never questioned or challenged. There were three primary reasons why people accepted his authority as an apostle of Jesus:

(1) **His close relationship with Jesus**. Along with John and James, Peter had been especially close to Jesus during his earthly life and ministry [Mark 9:2, 13:3, 14:33; Luke 22:8]. Peter was even allowed to see Jesus in his glory when he was temporarily transfigured [Matthew 17:1-13]. While all of the disciples (minus Judas) were with Jesus in the Garden of Gethsemane, just before his arrest, he only took Peter, James, and John with him to a further location where he prayed.

(2) **The soundness of his doctrine**. Beginning with his first public preaching assignment (as recorded in Acts 2:14-41), after having been baptized in the Holy Spirit, Peter skillfully and accurately connected Old Testament prophecies to the life of Jesus, proving that he was the Messiah. He preached convincingly and scripturally that the message of the cross of Christ was validated by God the Father as his work to reconcile man to himself. Peter did the same in Acts 3:11- 4:31; 5:29-42.

(3) **Miraculous signs and wonders associated with him**. As Peter used the keys of the kingdom of heaven to open the door for all

people—Jews, Samaritans, and Gentiles—God allowed miraculous signs to be displayed to cement into the minds of those present that the message was of God and not man: a sound like a violent wind and visible objects that looked like tongues of fire [Acts 2:1-3], the supernatural ability to speak in other languages neither learned nor previously spoken [Acts 2:4], and miraculous healings [Acts 3:1-10; 5:12-16].

In Acts 9, we are introduced to Saul of Tarsus. After his spiritual conversion, he went on to become the primary representative of Christ in the book of Acts and was used by God to author most of the New Testament letters. While Peter unlocked and opened the door of heaven to the Gentiles by preaching the gospel [I Corinthians 10], it was Paul whom God appointed as his handpicked representative [Acts 9:15] to walk through the door and go throughout the Gentile world to spread the message of the gospel of Jesus Christ.

Because of his life prior to submitting to the Lord Jesus Christ, Saul (Paul) was not initially accepted or trusted by followers of Jesus. Many did not know if his profession of faith was genuine, thinking that he might be using his supposed belief in Jesus as a ploy to infiltrate the church and resume his harsh persecution, imprisonment, and even execution of believers:

> When he came to Jerusalem, he (Saul) tried to join the
> disciples, but they were all afraid of him, not believing that

he really was a disciple. But Barnabas took him and brought him to the apostles. He told them how Saul on his journey had seen the Lord and that the Lord had spoken to him, and how in Damascus he had preached fearlessly in the name of Jesus. [Acts 9:26-27]

So, just as God validated Peter's apostleship and his calling, he also validated Paul's apostleship so that all would know that Paul was God's chosen vessel to carry Jesus' name before the Gentiles and their king and before the people of Israel. Remember that God incarnate, the Lord Jesus Christ, constantly dealt with people's unbelief and demands for signs to prove that he was who he said he was. He knew that Paul would deal with the same barrier of others' unbelief regarding his spiritual conversion and calling. Consider Paul's words to the Corinthians:

> So then, men ought to regard us as servants of Christ and as those entrusted with the secret things of God...Some of you have become arrogant, as if I were not coming to you. But I will come to you very soon, if the Lord is willing, and then I will find out not only how these arrogant people are talking, but what power they have. For the kingdom of God is not a matter of talk but of power. What do you prefer? Shall I come to you with a whip, or in love and with a gentle spirit? [I Corinthians 4:1;18-21]

Am I not free? Am I not an apostle? Have I not seen Jesus

our Lord? Are you not the result of my work in the Lord? Even though I may not be an apostle to others, surely I am to you! For you are the seal of my apostleship in the Lord. [I Corinthians 9:1-2]

I have made a fool of myself, but you drove me to it. I ought to have been commended by you, for I am not in the least inferior to the 'super-apostles,' even though I am nothing. The things that mark an apostle—signs, wonders and miracles—were done among you with great perseverance. [II Corinthians 12:11-12]

In his foreknowledge, knowing that Paul would endure these things, God did for him what he did for Peter, validating his call as an apostle of the Lord Jesus Christ. He did this in the same three ways as he did for Peter:

(1) **His close relationship with Jesus**. After Paul was converted and called by Jesus, as recorded in Acts 9:1-19, he went into Arabia and spent three years with revelation from Jesus (the same number of years that the other eleven apostles spent learning from Jesus). We read in Acts 18:9-11; 22:17-21; 23:11 that Jesus appeared and spoke to Paul often in his ministry. In II Corinthians 12:1-4, Paul shares that Jesus allowed him to see and hear things in heaven that man is not yet permitted to discuss.

(2) **The soundness of his doctrine**. In II Peter 3:15-16, Peter says,

"Bear in mind that our Lord's patience means salvation, just as our dear brother Paul also wrote you with the wisdom that God gave him. He writes the same way in all his letters, speaking in them of these matters. His letters contain some things that are hard to understand, which ignorant and unstable people distort, as they do other Scriptures, to their own destruction."

(3) **Miraculous signs and wonders associated with him**. Acts 19:1-7 details Paul's encounter with twelve disciples of John the Baptist who indicated that they were not yet born-again because they had not yet been indwelt by God's Spirit or even heard of the message of the Spirit. They needed the gospel of the Messiah (Christ) explained to them, so Paul did what he wrote about later in Romans 10:8-15. Having accepted Paul's message of Christ the Savior, the twelve men, former followers of Judaism, made the public profession of their inward belief and commitment to Jesus by being baptized in water. After this, Paul placed his hands on them—in the same way that Peter placed his hands on the Samaritans—and "the Holy Spirit came upon them, and they spoke in tongues (other languages) and prophesied." [Acts 19:5-7]. Acts 19:11-12 says, "God did extraordinary miracles through Paul, so that even handkerchiefs and aprons that had touched him were taken to the sick, and their illnesses were cured and the evil spirits left them." Again, God allowed this to both confirm Paul's authority as an apostle and validate his teaching. Note that the men received the gift of the Spirit when they trusted Christ Jesus as Savior—not after. The Bible makes it clear

that all people who submit to Jesus are instantaneously spiritually baptized in the Holy Spirit and become spiritually born-again.

In Galatians 3:2, Paul asks, "I would like to learn just one thing from you: did you receive the Spirit by observing the law, or by believing what you heard?" This was directed toward Christians who, after having been saved by grace through faith and not by works/human effort [Ephesians 2:8,9], were now trying to achieve spiritual maturity by human efforts/works [Galatians 3:3-5]. In verses 2 and 5 of Galatians 3, Paul states that the Galatians, like all others redeemed by God, were given (received) the Holy Spirit when they believed what they heard—the gospel of the Lord Jesus Christ. There was no second work of grace they had to pursue.

Chapter Seven

The Message of the Cross and God's Heavenly Stamp of Approval

In previous chapters, it was scripturally verified that Jesus appointed Peter as his apostle to use the keys of the kingdom of God (the Lord's truth, authority, and power) to open the door of faith to Jews, Samaritans, and Gentiles. Peter's message was clear and consistent to each of these three people groups:

> Men of Israel, listen to this: Jesus of Nazareth was a man accredited by God to you by miracles, wonders and signs, which God did among you through him, as you yourselves know. This man was handed over to you by God's set purpose and foreknowledge; and you, with the help of wicked men, put him to death by nailing him to the cross. But God raised him from the dead, freeing him from the agony of death, because it was impossible for death to keep its hold on him.... Therefore let all Israel be assured of this: God has made this Jesus, whom you crucified, both Lord and Christ. [Acts 2:22-24; 36]

Similarly, it is clear from the Bible that Jesus appointed Paul to be his apostle to the Gentiles, sharing with them the same gospel message that Peter had:

> The God who made the world and everything in it is the Lord of heaven and earth and does not live in temples built by hands. And he is not served by human hands, as if he needed anything, because he himself gives all men life and breath and everything else...In the past God overlooked such ignorance, but now he commands all people everywhere to repent. For he has set a day when he will judge the world with justice by the man he has appointed. He has given proof of this to all men by raising him from the dead. [Acts 17:24-31]

Scripture informs us that while some Jews, Samaritans, and Gentiles believed the messages Peter, Paul, and others preached, many did not believe due to their unbelief. Unbelief in what? For the Jews, unbelief that Jesus was their Messiah and would also redeem Gentiles, giving them the same inheritance. For the Gentiles, unbelief centered around the message's seeming lack of credibility (most were not familiar with the Hebrew Scriptures) and their human wisdom failing to grasp the simple message of the cross:

> For the message of the cross is foolishness to those who are perishing, but to us who are being saved it is the power of God...For the Jews require a sign, and the Greeks [Gentiles] seek after wisdom, but we preach Christ crucified, unto the Jews a stumbling block, and unto the Greeks foolishness. [I Corinthians 1:18, 22-23]

In his omniscience, God knew this and publicly testified to Jesus' Messiahship and the legitimacy of the gospel preached by Peter, Paul, and others per the legal requirements of the law given to the Jews—that two or three witnesses were needed to confirm the legitimacy of matters. How and when did God get on the witness stand, and how did he provide his testimony? Hebrews 2:3-4 provides the answer:

> Shall we escape if we ignore so great a salvation? This salvation, which was first announced by the Lord (Jesus), was confirmed to us by those (his apostles) who heard him. God also testified to it by signs, wonders and various miracles, and gifts of the Holy Spirit distributed according to his will.

So, Scripture informs us that God the Father testified from heaven by providing signs, wonders and various miracles, and gifts of the Holy Spirit. In Acts 2:22, Peter tells his listeners that God the Father testified to the truth that Jesus was the Savior by miracles, wonders, and signs—which he did through him:

> "Fellow Israelites, listen to this: Jesus of Nazareth was a man accredited by God to you by miracles, wonders and signs, which God did among you through him, as you yourselves know."

So, Peter verified that God the Father gave divine testimony to the

61

truth of the gospel through supernatural means - done by both the Son of God and his chosen ambassadors.

The sole purpose of the miracles, wonders, signs, and gifts of the Holy Spirit poured out by God was to validate to all—whether Jews, Samaritans, or Gentiles—that the message preached by Jesus and confirmed by his apostles and disciples was, indeed, from God. In doing this, God upheld the requirement of his law: "Every matter must be established by the testimony of two or three witnesses" [II Corinthians 13:1].

Consistent with the definition of the word "sign," which is "a gesture or action used to convey information or instructions," God testified to the truth of the message of salvation in Jesus by heaven-sent signs. Understanding this purpose for sign gifts from God will prove very helpful as this study progresses.

Thus far, we have studied key passages in the book of Acts that lay out God's plan and purpose for miracles and gifts of the Holy Spirit—particularly in the context of salvation. The next step in our exploration will be to examine I Corinthians to dig deeper into the baptism of the Holy Spirit in the lives of believers and study the gift of tongues. It is important to note that throughout the letters of I and II Corinthians, the apostle Paul had to instruct, rebuke, and correct the Corinthians in many ways due to their previous lives of unbounded lust, extreme sensuality, idol worship, and rampant immorality. The city was filled with temples dedicated to idols and false gods, with one of the most influential ones being the temple dedicated to Aphrodite, the Greek goddess of love. The worship of Aphrodite promoted sex rituals (prostitution) in the name of religion. It is estimated that at the height of Aphrodite's influence in Corinth, about 1,000 "sacred" prostitutes served in the temple. With all the spiritual confusion and emotional baggage that individuals in Corinth grew up with, it is no surprise that many new Corinthian believers had to be reminded by Paul to jettison worldly passions and unbiblical practices that brought them (rather than God) attention, pleasure, and esteem. This included their improper understanding and exercising of spiritual gifts.

Chapter Eight

Spiritual Gifts: Real and Counterfeit

Now about spiritual gifts, brothers, I do not want you to
be ignorant. [I Corinthians 12:1]

I Corinthians 7:1 informs us that the Corinthians had written to Paul concerning several topics they had questions about, such as marriage (chapter seven) and food sacrificed to idols (chapter eight). In chapter twelve, he begins to address their questions about spiritual gifts. Ignorance, defined as a lack of information/knowledge or understanding, is revealed in one's life by either failing to act or taking improper action regarding some issue. This is what the apostle Paul was addressing among the Christians living in Corinth regarding their understanding of why God gives spiritual gifts. His aim in answering their questions about spiritual gifts was to provide truth, correct erroneous thinking and actions among the followers of Jesus, and set them on paths for living fruitful lives unto God—according to truth and order, not deception and chaos [I Corinthians 14:33].

Similarly today, there is much confusion among Christians regarding spiritual gifts. However, when we have sincere hearts and devotion to God's truth, the holy Scriptures bring clarity to the baptism of the Holy Spirit, speaking in tongues, and the purpose of sign gifts. With soberness of mind and peace in our hearts, we must remember that God is neither confused nor conflicted about these topics.

The Corinthians believers to whom Paul was writing were formerly idol worshippers:

> You know that when you were pagans, somehow or other you were influenced and led astray to mute idols. [I Corinthians 12:2]

Because of their spiritual immaturity, he wrote the following words:

> Therefore, my dear friends, flee from idolatry. I speak to sensible people; judge for yourselves what I say…Consider the people of Israel: Do not those who eat the sacrifices participate in the altar? Do I mean then that a sacrifice offered to an idol is anything, or that an idol is anything? No, but the sacrifices of pagans are offered to demons, not to God, and I do not want you to be participants with demons. You cannot drink the cup of the Lord and the cup of demons too; you cannot have a part in both the Lord's table and the table of demons. Are we trying to arouse the Lord's jealousy? Are we stronger than he? [I Corinthians 10:14-15;18-22]

Satan always takes the truth of God and twists it, using deception to steer both seekers and followers of God off the path of truth. Because Corinth had scores of temples dedicated to the worship of pagan gods and goddesses (such as Apollo, Asclepius, Aphrodite, and others), Satan's wicked influence in the city's culture was pervasive and deeply rooted. Paul reminded the Corinthian believers that behind the worship of inanimate physical idols are actually demons and instructed them with the following in II Corinthians 6:14-17:

> Do not be yoked together with unbelievers. For what do righteousness and wickedness have in common? Or what fellowship can light have with darkness? What harmony is there between Christ and Belial? Or what does a believer have in common with an unbeliever? What agreement is there between the temple of God and idols? For we are the temple of the living God. As God has said: "I will live with them and walk among them, and I will be their God, and they will be my people." Therefore, "Come out from them and be separate, says the Lord. Touch no unclean thing, and I will receive you."

The instruction to not be yoked together with unbelievers was highly important because many Corinthian believers had followed pagan religious rituals before submitting their lives to Jesus. Paul was warning them not to fall prey to ungodly beliefs and practices characterized by the idol worship in Corinth:

> Therefore I tell you that no one who is speaking by the Spirit of God says, "Jesus be cursed," and no one can say, "Jesus is Lord," except by the Holy Spirit. [I Corinthians

12:3]

Paul addressed the fact that many people professed to be Christians, yet, when pressure from the culture (family, friends, etc.) came upon them, they recanted—turning away from their professed allegiance to Jesus. Jesus addressed this in a parable recorded in Matthew 13:20-21:

> The one who received the seed that fell on rocky places is the man who hears the word and at once receives it with joy. But since he has no root, he lasts only a short time. When trouble or persecution comes because of the word, he quickly falls away.

All who hear God's truth and confess (come into agreement with God) that Jesus is who he says he is (God incarnate) can only do so by the conviction and leading of the Holy Spirit. Without spiritual rebirth/regeneration, nobody can say from their heart, demonstrated by obedience and exaltation of Christ, that Jesus is Lord:

> The man without the Spirit does not accept the things that come from the Spirit of God, for they are foolishness to him, and he cannot understand them, because they are spiritually discerned. [I Corinthians 2:14]

> The god of this age has blinded the minds of unbelievers, so that they cannot see the light of the gospel of the glory

of Christ, who is the image of God. [II Corinthians 4:4]

God's Purpose in Giving Spiritual Gifts

In I Corinthians 12:4-6, Paul shifts to explaining the true origin and purpose of spiritual gifts:

> There are different kinds of gifts, but the same Spirit. There are different kinds of service, but the same Lord. There are different kinds of working, but the same God works all of them in all men.

God is the giver of spiritual gifts and predetermined, before the foundation of the world, both the call and gift(s) that he would give to each believer—for his glory, honor, and praise. So a logical question is this: what is he trying to achieve by giving his followers spiritual gifts and kingdom work assignments? Jesus provides the answer, informing us in Matthew 16:18 that God's the purpose in giving spiritual gifts to those who are born-again is to build his church, which equates to seeing people become spiritually born-again and grow as his disciples. His church is not a physical building but the collective and massive group of people from every tribe, tongue (language), and nation who have placed their eternal trust in Christ Jesus as Lord and Savior. The apostle Paul reaffirms this in Ephesians 4:11-13 as the reason why the Spirit of God gives all Christians at least one spiritual gift when they are born-again and added to the church (body) of Jesus Christ:

It was he who gave some to be apostles, some to be prophets, some to be evangelists, and some to be pastors and teachers, to prepare God's people for works of service, so that the body of Christ may be built up. Until we all reach unity in the faith and in the knowledge of the Son of God and become mature, attaining to the whole measure of the fullness of Christ.

Chapter Nine

Spiritual Gifts: Given by God, Not Obtained by Man

Now to each one the manifestation *of the Spirit is given
for the common good. [I Corinthians 12:7]*

The key to understanding God's Word with depth of insight for effective living is this: allow Scripture, line upon line and precept upon precept, to answer/interpret itself. I Corinthians 12:7 states clearly that God's purpose in giving Christians spiritual gifts (referred to as "the manifestation of the Spirit") is for the common good—not for individual/personal edification. This truth is reinforced in Paul's letters to other churches, as well:

> Then we will no longer be infants, tossed back and forth by
> the waves, and blown here and there by every wind of
> teaching and by the cunning and craftiness of men in their
> deceitful scheming. Instead, speaking the truth in love, we
> will in all things grow up into him who is the Head, that is,
> Christ. From him the whole body, joined and held together
> by every supporting ligament, grows and builds itself up in
> love, as each part does its work. [Ephesians 4:14-16]

This will be important to remember as we move along throughout chapters 12–14 of I Corinthians. First, let's look at I Corinthians 12:8-11:

> To one there is given through the Spirit the message of wisdom, to another the message of knowledge by means of the same Spirit, to another faith by the same Spirit, to another gifts of healing by that one Spirit, to another miraculous powers, to another prophecy, to another distinguishing between spirits, to another speaking in different kinds of tongues, and to still another the interpretation of tongues. All these are the work of one and the same Spirit, and he gives them to each one, just as he determines.

Again, the Bible is quite clear on the distribution of the spiritual gifts to believers by the Spirit of God. Verses 8-10 tell us, in no uncertain terms, that each person has a gift(s) given to them as God sees fit, according to his eternal plan of building his church. If what is said in verses 8-10 seems unclear, verse 11 brings home the point: "he (the Spirit of God) gives them (gifts from the Spirit of God) to each one (Christians), just as he (the Spirit of God) determines." Based on this revelation, the prevalent teaching that all Christians should/must have one particular gift is refuted.

[Reminder: Verses 12 and 13 of I Corinthians 12 were discussed in detail in Chapter 1 of this book as the baptism of the Holy Spirit was explored and explained contextually from Scripture.]

Chapter Ten

Spiritual Gifts: Purpose-Given
for Mature Living

The apostle Paul wrote to the Corinthians to address issues of pride and insecurity that arose in their church due to the misuse and abuse of spiritual gifts that God had given:

> Now the body is not made up of one part but of many. If the foot should say, "Because I am not a hand, I do not belong to the body," it would not for that reason cease to be part of the body. And if the ear should say, "Because I am not an eye, I do not belong to the body," it would not for that reason cease to be part of the body. If the whole body were an eye, where would the sense of hearing be? If the whole body were an ear, where would the sense of smell be? But in fact God has arranged the parts in the body, every one of them, just as he wanted them to be. If they were all one part, where would the body be? As it is, there are many parts, but one body. The eye cannot say to the hand, "I don't need you!" And the head cannot say to the feet, "I don't need you!" On the contrary, those parts of the body that seem to be weaker are indispensable, and the parts that we think are less honorable we treat with special honor. And the parts that are unpresentable are treated with special

modesty, while our presentable parts need no special treatment. But God has combined the members of the body and has given greater honor to the parts that lacked it, so that there should be no division in the body, but that its parts should have equal concern for each other. [I Cor. 12:15-24]

While one gift (such as preaching/teaching) may be more outwardly evidenced and applauded than another (such as administration or hospitality), they have the same value in God's eyes. What matters to God is not the type of gift given. Rather, he looks at the individual's attitude and faithfulness in dispensing the gift for his eternal purposes. The Lord's rewards for faithful living and obedience have nothing to do with the gift in and of themselves. He rewards faith and obedience.

God arranges the parts in the body of Christ to accomplish his sovereign purposes. He is the one who dispenses gifts to each regenerated believer by his Spirit's selection [I Cor. 12:8-11]. He is not a respecter of persons or gifts (that he gives)—and neither should we be.

In verses 27-31, the apostle lists the hierarchy of spiritual gifts that God had given:

Now you are the body of Christ, and each one of you is a part of it. And in the church God has appointed first of all apostles, second prophets, third teachers, then workers of miracles, also those having gifts of healing, those able to help others, those with gifts of administration, and those speaking in different kinds of tongues. Are all apostles? Are all prophets? Are all teachers? Do all work miracles? Do all have gifts of healing? Do all speak in tongues? Do all interpret? But eagerly desire the greater gifts. [I Corinthians 12:27-31]

God ranked the gifts in order of importance to the church's authority, truth, transformational power, effectiveness, and validity—their ability to win people to saving faith in Jesus Christ and then disciple them to walk in obedience to God's Word.

Verse 28 reveals that the first gift of importance to God, which he gave to a specific group of men, was the special appointment of apostles of Jesus. The twelve men to whom he gave this gift were personally taught by Jesus and directly assigned by him to carry out certain tasks related to building the foundation of the church of God.

The second gift that God distributed to certain people by his Spirit was the gift of prophecy, specifically for the delivery of the Word of God according to the new covenant (New Testament).

The third gift in God's hierarchy of importance regarding the construction of his church is teachers. We are informed in the Bible that the church's primary purpose is to teach the people of God the

Word of God so that they might know and obey God's truth as effective ambassadors of Christ in a lost world.

These first three gifts administered by God, in order of their importance in establishing a solid foundation for building the church of Jesus Christ, are echoed again by Paul to the Ephesians believers:

> So Christ himself gave the apostles, the prophets, the evangelists, the pastors and teachers, to equip his people for works of service, so that the body of Christ may be built up until we all reach unity in the faith and in the knowledge of the Son of God and become mature, attaining to the whole measure of the fullness of Christ. Then we will no longer be infants, tossed back and forth by the waves, and blown here and there by every wind of teaching and by the cunning and craftiness of people in their deceitful scheming. Instead, speaking the truth in love, we will grow to become in every respect the mature body of him who is the head, that is, Christ. From him the whole body, joined and held together by every supporting ligament, grows and builds itself up in love, as each part does its work. [Ephesians 4:11-16]

Please note that in this passage, the word "then" begins verse 14, signifying the vital role that the three gifts just discussed play in developing mature people of God who can effectively carry out his work. "Then" signifies that when the first five gifts listed are exercised in growing the body of Christ, the result is believers who are no longer infants in the faith, blown here and there by every wind of teaching.

Verses 29 and 30 of I Corinthians 12 indicate that the Holy Spirit does not give everyone all the spiritual gifts. As discussed during the review of I Corinthians 12:7-11, no person determines the gift(s) that they will receive from God's Spirit. Rather, the Holy Spirit sovereignly chooses to grant spiritual gifts to each member of the body of Christ as he determines—to fulfill his purposes in maturing the body of Christ and accomplishing his plans on the earth. Grasping this truth will prove invaluable as we explore and contemplate I Corinthians 12-14.

Chapter Eleven

(Spiritual Gifts) – (Love) = Nothing

The Language of Love

If I speak in the tongues of men and of angels, but have not love, I am only a resounding gong or a clanging cymbal. If I have the gift of prophecy and can fathom all mysteries and all knowledge, and if I have a faith that can move mountains, but have not love, I am nothing. If I give all I possess to the poor and surrender my body to the flames, but have not love, I gain nothing. [I Corinthians 13:1-3]

I Corinthians 13 has been referred to by some as "Paul's Hymn of Love." It is one of the most well-known passages of Scripture in the world, widely read at marriages—even by couples who profess no real love for God or belief in the Bible. The words of this chapter intuitively draw people to conclude that Paul was speaking to and about individuals in romantic relationships. However, this is not the case. The context and chief goal of this chapter was to instruct the members of the Corinthian church on how to act toward one another as they exercised spiritual gifts.

God had Paul write the words of I Corinthians 13 as a pause between chapters 12 and 14, in which he provides both instruction and rebuke regarding the Corinthians' use of the spiritual gifts of tongues. This definitive chapter was given to Paul by inspiration from the Holy Spirit to instruct the believers in Corinth that love must be at the root of whatever a believer in Christ purposes to say and do for the glory of God—including the exercising of spiritual gifts.

In I Corinthians 13:1-3, Paul states that exercising spiritual gifts without sincere love yields nothing that promotes the spiritual edification of others, the glorification of God, and praise/rewards from God. The four spiritual gifts that he mentions are:

- **Speaking** to others (no matter what language is used) about the truths of God [I Cor. 13:1]
- **Prophesying** words of knowledge and discerning mysteries by God's Spirit [I Cor. 13:2]
- **Faith** to trust God to do miraculous things [I Cor. 13:2]
- **Giving** of oneself or one's resources, no matter how great the sacrifice [I Cor. 13:3]

Why were these four spiritual gifts the focus of his correction? First, it is because when exercised, these gifts naturally draw attention to the person(s) through whom God allows them to emanate. Thus, Paul had to address the pride that was developing in the hearts of many. Secondly, the first twelve chapters of I Corinthians reveal the rampant idolatry associated with these particular gifts that was at the root of their needed correction and rebuke.

Many Corinthian church members were either abusing the four aforementioned gifts or pretending to have them. They were still allowing various practices and habits of Corinth's ungodly culture to infect their minds, causing the following thorns of the flesh to manifest: divisions (1:10-17), pride and boasting (1:18-31; 5:6-7), showing off their tongue-speaking and prophetic abilities (2:1-16), immaturity, jealousy, quarreling, self-deception because of pride (3:1-23), arrogance (4:18), sexual immorality (5:1-2), disputes and lawsuits among each other (6:1-7), various immoral behaviors such as cheating, sexual immorality, homosexuality, thievery, drunkenness, slander, swindling (6:8-11), sex with prostitutes (6:15-16), not bridling their freedoms and causing others to sin in the area of idolatry (8:1-13; 10:14-33), criticizing Paul and rejecting his apostleship (9:1-18), rejecting God's spiritual order in relationships (11:1-16), and abusing the Lord's Supper (11:17-34). Wow, these were serious issues! The Corinthians had indeed been wrapped up in the sinful culture of their day and not living sanctified lives. The words of Paul to the Corinthian believers in chapter 11, verse 17 sum up their need for correction regarding their abuse of the Lord's Supper: "In the following directives I have no praise for you, for your meetings do more harm than good."

What's Love Got to Do with It? Everything!

In I Corinthians 13:4-13, Paul paints one of the most beautiful and descriptive pictures of love that the world has ever known. He tells the Corinthian believers that this selfless and God-generated love should be what drives their desire to speak, prophesy, perform miraculous acts of faith, and sacrificially give their money, resources, and even life in the name of the Lord Jesus Christ. This driver of love was opposed to the wayward motivations of the carnal Corinthians, listed in verses 4 through 6 as envy, boasting, pride, rudeness, self-seeking, anger, evil, distrustfulness, and not enduring. In verse 11, Paul even tells them that it is time to grow up and stop acting childish.

Now that we understand why Paul had to write I Corinthians 13—to show them the most excellent way of living and ministering [I Corinthians 12:31(b)]—let's examine the first verse of this chapter as it relates to the baptism of the Holy Spirit and speaking in tongues:

> If I speak in the tongues of men and of angels, but have not love, I am only a resounding gong or a clanging cymbal. [I Corinthians 13:1]

Unfortunately, most people reading I Corinthians 13:1 err in at least one of two ways when attempting to decipher its context and meaning. First, most inadvertently believe that the primary focus of this verse is tongues. However, as stated in previous paragraphs, the focus is love. Paul states that if he (or anyone else) endeavors to speak to others about anything—most importantly, the oracles of

God—yet has no desire to genuinely connect with his hearers in love, then those hearers will most likely not benefit from what is said.

The word "tongues" is found only twice in I Corinthians 13, mentioned in verse 1 as being ineffective without love and in verse 8 as being temporary and not everlasting. On the contrary, the word "love" is mentioned eight times in I Corinthians 13 and is also referred to as "it" another eight times, proving it to be the overwhelming and clear focus of the chapter. The apostle Paul affirms that this love chapter is the glue holding together the spiritual gift chapters of 12 and 14.

The second misunderstanding that many have regarding I Corinthians 13:1 is to assume that Paul is referring to two different types of tongues (languages): the tongues of men and the tongues of angels. Note, however, that the verse does not read, "If I speak in the tongues of men and the tongues of angels." That sentence structure would indeed make it clear that there are many languages of men (from different regions and countries) and that there are many languages of angels.

Let's put our thinking caps on as we consider what we see in the Bible from Genesis to Revelation: angels, and God himself, spoke to men and women in Scripture on many occasions—and always in the known languages of those people. None of the many people spoken to by God and angels in the Old Testament were born-again, having the Holy Spirit resident in them. Thus, they could not have had the gift of either speaking in or interpreting foreign tongues. Yet, they spoke to and understood these heavenly beings because the tongues (languages) spoken by the angels were known earthly languages, just like all the languages spoken at Pentecost by the early disciples.

When translated to heaven in an experience that led him to write the Book of Revelation, the apostle John heard the Lord Jesus speak to him, communicated directly with angels and heard multitudes of them talk and sing, and heard throngs of people in the heavenly realm from every nation and tongue (human languages) singing praises to God. Never once do the Scriptures indicate that what John heard was angels and people speaking and singing in a heavenly tongue(s) that was incoherent or needed translation. Also, they were not saying esoteric or deep things that the human mind and languages cannot grasp. Their words were sound instruction, praise, or prophesy/judgment of what was to come.

So, as we once again contemplate the meaning of the words of I Corinthians 13:1 with proper contextual interpretation, we understand Paul to be saying that the audible utterances of the profound and deep oracles of God spoken by men or angels, regardless of the language or messenger, fall on deaf ears without the edifying ingredient of love. Still, there are valid questions. Is there an exclusive language(s) spoken in the heavenly realm that is different from human languages? What language did Adam and Eve speak, and was that the language God gave to angels? Well, the accurate response to these questions is this: we don't know. What we do know is that the Bible tells us that God is Spirit, and his worshipers must worship him in the Spirit and in truth [John 4:24]. However, worshiping in the Spirit has nothing to do with humans speaking audible words to him. David declares in Psalm 139:4:

> Before a word is on my tongue you, Lord, know it completely.

Because of his foreknowledge and omniscience, God does not need a person to say anything, whether in their native language or foreign, for him to know their thoughts, feelings, and intentions. There are numerous occasions in the Old Testament when God or angels spoke to humans, and there is no indication in Scripture that there was a mysterious heavenly language spoken that had to be translated for the hearers to understand. In Job 1:6-12, it is written that angels went before the throne to present themselves to God, and Satan did as well. The dialogue between God and Satan, like all other incidents where God or angels are recorded in the Bible as talking with others, is always relayed in known tongues (languages of mankind) and never as a heavenly spiritual language that had to be translated for humans.

When Christians speak, it should be characterized by sincerity and edifying love with the purpose of creating transformation in the hearer's understanding and life. God's main purpose in leading Paul to write I Corinthians 13 was to remind the immature, worldly, and wayward Corinthian Christians that living a life of love is what they should desire above all other things. The primary purpose of Christians is to exalt the Lord in their hearts as the central focus of who they are, what they do, and why they do it (their affections, desires, motives, actions):

> One of the teachers of the law came and heard them debating. Noticing that Jesus had given them a good answer, he asked him, "Of all the commandments, which is the most important?" "The most important one," answered Jesus, "is this: 'Hear, O Israel: The Lord our God, the Lord is one. Love the Lord your God with all your heart and with all your soul and with all your mind and with all your strength.'" [Mark 12:28-30]

The second purpose of Christians is to minister to others by caring for them and meeting their physical, emotional, mental, and spiritual needs as much as possible:

> "The second is this: 'Love your neighbor as yourself.' There is no commandment greater than these." [Mark 12:31]

In addition to discussing the important aspect of love in I Corinthian 13, Paul introduces a topic that he will dive into with more detail in chapter 14: confusion regarding the spiritual gift of speaking in tongues. He addresses both the purpose and abuses of tongues occurring among the Corinthian Christians, reiterating that order, not chaos, characterizes the gifts and purposes of God.

Chapter Twelve

Love... God's Perfect Gift Wrap

Love is patient, love is kind. It does not envy, it does not boast, it is not proud. It is not rude, it is not self-seeking, it is not easily angered, it keeps no record of wrongs. Love does not delight in evil but rejoices with the truth. It always protects, always trusts, always hopes, always perseveres. [I Corinthians 13:4-7]

The verses above will sound familiar to those who have attended weddings. It has been *the* section of the Bible invariably read by scores of wedding officials across the globe when conducting wedding ceremonies and discussing the bond of love between a husband and wife. Beyond its vital importance in marriage, love is the all-important factor in every aspect of life. Because all people are in unions of relationships with others—at home, work, and play—the selfless love described in the preceding verses is what mature and loving people live and give to others. Paul had to write these things because this type of love was not being demonstrated among the Corinthian believers.

Love never fails. But where there are prophecies, they will cease; where there are tongues, they will be stilled; where there is knowledge, it will pass away. For we know in part

89

and we prophesy in part... [I Corinthians 13:8-9]

In the first sentence of verse 8, the apostle Paul sums up the eternal nature and reliability of love, stating that it never fails. On the contrary, for the remainder of verse 8 and verse 9, he references the temporary nature of the three sign gifts of future-telling prophecy, tongues, and knowledge (that which would not naturally be known). He states quite clearly that some spiritual gifts would one day end and no longer be needed:

> But when perfection comes, the imperfect disappears. [I Corinthians 13:10]

God is perfect and is the very essence of love. The Bible tells us in I John 4:16(b)-21:

> God is love. Whoever lives in love lives in God, and God in him. In this way, love is made complete among us so that we will have confidence on the day of judgment, because in this world we are like him. There is no fear in love. But perfect love drives out fear, because fear has to do with punishment. The one who fears is not made perfect in love. We love because he first loved us. If anyone says, 'I love God,' yet hates his brother, he is a liar. For anyone who does not love his brother, whom he has seen, cannot love God, whom he has not seen. And he has given us this command: Whoever loves God must also love his brother.

Re-read I Corinthians 13:10. Do you see the correlation between that verse and the truth found in I John 4? Jesus Christ is the Perfect One. He is the defining standard and sole source of love. Thus, there is only one reason the Spirit of God gives some Christians the temporary spiritual gifts of prophecy/words of knowledge and tongues: to present the truth of God's Word to others so that they may come to know him who is eternal and have his love abide within them. Sadly, due to a lack of seeking God in a consistent, intentional, and committed way, many Christ-followers talk, think, reason, and act in spiritually immature ways:

> When I was a child, I talked like a child, I thought like a child, I reasoned like a child. When I became a man, I put childish ways behind me. Now we see but a poor reflection as in a mirror; then we shall see face to face. Now I know in part; then I shall know fully, even as I am fully known. And now these three remain: faith, hope and love. But the greatest of these is love. [I Corinthians 13:11-13]

If, however, the words of Matthew 6:33-34 are lived out in increasing measure in a Christian's life, then spiritual wisdom, maturity, and a greater reliance on God will be the result:

> But seek first his kingdom and his righteousness, and all these things will be given to you as well. Therefore do not worry about tomorrow, for tomorrow will worry about itself. Each day has enough trouble of its own. [Matthew

6:33-34]

Place your faith in God! He will give you the hope that you need to conquer all circumstances by filling you with his love.

Chapter Thirteen

Unraveling the Mystery

Follow the way of love and eagerly desire spiritual gifts,
especially the gift of prophecy. [I Corinthians 14:1]

The words of I Corinthians 14:1 were written as a bridge to reconnect Paul's Corinthian audience to the last verse of I Corinthians 12, which reads:

> Now eagerly desire the greater gifts. And yet I will show you
> the most excellent way. [I Corinthians 12:31]

In verses 27-30 of chapter 12, Paul listed the spiritual gifts deemed by the Holy Spirit as most important, which all relate to the revelation and teaching of God's Word. In the last sentence of chapter 12, Paul tells the Corinthians to eagerly desire to have and exercise the greater gifts but to do so in the most excellent way (love). In the first verse of chapter 14, he reiterates that the Corinthians should follow the way of love and eagerly desire spiritual gifts—the greater gift being the gift of prophecy (speaking the oracles of God). So, we see that the two verses that sandwich "the love chapter" (I Corinthians 13) are identical in content.

The Greek word used for prophecy in I Corinthians 12:31 and 14:1

is *prophēteuō*, a verb with the primary meaning of (1) telling forth the divine counsels (God's known Word) or (2) foretelling the future. Paul admonished the Corinthians to desire, most of all, the gift of prophecy. Why? The most miraculous, life-changing, and impactful thing one can do for another person is to share God's holy Word with them—allowing it to penetrate their inner being (soul/mind) and bring transformation from the inside-out:

> For the word of God is alive and active. Sharper than any double-edged sword, it penetrates even to dividing soul and spirit, joints and marrow; it judges the thoughts and attitudes of the heart. [Hebrews 4:12]

A Mystery Heavenly Language?

> For anyone who speaks in a tongue does not speak to men but to God. Indeed, no one understands him; he utters mysteries with his spirit. [I Corinthians 14:2]

To successfully wade through various teachings on the spiritual gifts, specifically those related to our study of speaking in tongues, we must understand (1) **God's purpose** for distributing spiritual gifts and (2) **the context** of the verses being examined. Here are some key reminders from I Corinthians 12:

- **I Corinthians 12:7** – God's purpose in giving all believers spiritual gifts is for the common good, to edify and strengthen the body of believers.

- **I Corinthians 12:8-10** – God gives each believer at least one spiritual gift.
- **I Corinthians 12:11,30(b)** – Only certain people, selected by the Holy Spirit, will ever be given the gift of tongues.

With these guiding truths, let's find out what the first half of I Corinthians 14:2, which states, "For anyone who speaks in a tongue does not speak to men but to God," really means. The question at hand is this: does tongues refer to a mysterious heavenly language spoken by God, other heavenly beings, and select born-again believers who have been given this gift by the Holy Spirit or does it mean something else?

Prayer is most simply defined as the act of communicating with God. When people aim to communicate with other people, they generally do it with words, speaking to them in a language that is understood by all who are present. Going beyond the use of words, one can also use sign language or various gestures to communicate with others. These outward forms of communication (audible words or physical movements) emanate from people's silent and unseen inner thoughts. It is the same with communication between a human and God. When believers "talk" to God, the true essence of their communication is not based on the expression of audible words or physical gestures but, rather, the inner motives, thoughts, and intents of the heart. God does not need to hear any audible expressions from people's mouths or see physical gestures from them to know their thoughts, feelings, and desires. (Read I Samuel 1:9-20, I Samuel 16:7, and Hebrews 4:13.) This truth calls for a re-examination of the teaching that tongues is a mystical, heavenly language used for "self-edification" and "deeper intimacy with God."

FIRST, as stated several times in God's Word, not all believers in Christ will receive the gift of tongues [I Corinthians 12:11,30]. If, indeed, speaking in tongues was the way to get "closer to God"—a supernatural heavenly language for developing more intimacy in communion with God—then God would be proven to be an unfair Father who shows favoritism only to the certain believers who are given this gift. Only these recipients of the gift of tongues would have access to the deeper riches of his grace, peace, joy, and contentment. Furthermore, this means no mute person could ever get close to him through the blessing of tongues.

SECOND, the context of the verses in I Corinthians 12 and 13 that have led up to chapter 14:2 indicate that the purpose of spiritual gifts is to edify the body of Christ. As reviewed, the tongues spoken at Pentecost [Acts 2:5-12] were known human dialects of the world — not a spiritual language that believers used to communicate with God. Furthermore, let's remember that Paul is writing all of this in response to the Corinthians' questions about doctrines and topics that were confusing them.

In the first sentence of his response in I Corinthians 14:2, Paul states that anyone speaking in a tongue (some human dialect) not known to his or her listeners in the congregation is, thus, understandable only to God. Imagine if you went to a work conference to learn about the latest technology related to your job, and the presenters spoke in a language you do not know. Similarly, consider how you would feel if you drove five hours to attend a concert, but the songs were sung in languages foreign to you. Lastly, imagine you're at a church service and the guest preacher from a foreign country gives an opening prayer to God in his native language that nobody else in the congregation knows. He would truly be speaking to God, but nobody else would be able to say "Amen," which means "I agree/so be it," because no one knows what has been said. The preacher knows and has been edified, with the satisfaction of communing with God in prayer, but what he prayed would be an utter mystery to all others present.

A Raucous from Bacchus

The context of the second half of I Corinthians 14:2 connects to what was going on in Corinth at the time of Paul's writing. Corinth was a city that, as we've reviewed, was hedonistic (sensual and pleasure-driven), immoral, and filled with demonic practices. Originating in Roman legend and worshiped in Corinth, Bacchus (Dionysus for the Greeks) was a party god. In fact, a drunken orgy is still referred to as a "bacchanalia." Devotees of Bacchus whipped themselves into a frenzy of intoxication, and in the spring, Roman women attended secret pleasure ceremonies in his name. Bacchus was associated with fertility, wine and grapes, and sexual free-for-alls. Bacchus, or rather the demon behind this fictitious god/idol, supposedly had a divine mission: the role of "liberator." During drunken frenzies, Bacchus would "liberate" people by loosening the tongues of those who were partakers of wine and other intoxicants, allowing them to be "free" to say and do what they wished. Paul was dealing with the fact that many of the Corinthian women (and men) who were now in the church, just out of paganism, were still imitating this pagan practice. The result was that observers (both Christian and non-Christians) would understand them to be either intoxicated with the spirits or crazy. Paul was erecting a wall between the true Christian experience of biblical tongues and the pagan practice associated with Bacchus, bringing truth and order out of error and chaos. Paul hammers his point even further in verse 9, as we will read soon.

Chapter Fourteen

Prophecy > Tongues Without Interpretation

But everyone who prophesies speaks to men for their strengthening, encouragement and comfort. He who speaks in a tongue edifies himself, but he who prophesies edifies the church. [I Corinthians 14:3-4]

In both I Corinthians 12:7 and Ephesians 4:11-16, the apostle Paul states the purpose for which spiritual gifts are given to people who are born-again: to strengthen, encourage, and comfort other believers in Christ so that they may reach spiritual maturity and grow in unity. Verses 3 and 4 of I Corinthians 14 reiterate this truth about the purpose of spiritual gifts—even the gift of speaking in a tongue.

Years ago, I was a speaker at the Mid-Atlantic Chinese Christian Conference, held in Lynchburg, Virginia. Throughout the weekend, Bible classes and presentations were given in Mandarin, Cantonese, and English. I led a few youth/young adult sessions in English on Friday and Saturday. On Sunday morning, all 500+ attendees gathered for the combined church service, for which I was the preacher. This morning service was successful ONLY because there were interpreters. Imagine if my opening prayer, spoken in English and filled with words of gratitude for all that had been done throughout the weekend thus far, had NOT been accompanied with translation. What would have been the result? Verse 4 of I Corinthians 14 tells us! The English-speaking participants and I would have been edified, rejoicing in giving God thanks for what he had done, but about 300 others would not have been able to rejoice and praise God. They would not have understood anything I was saying. Without translation at that Sunday service, there would have been no strengthening, encouragement, or comfort given to most of the congregation by my speaking.

> I would like every one of you to speak in tongues, but I would rather have you prophesy. He who prophesies is greater than one who speaks in tongues, unless he interprets, so that the church may be edified. [I Corinthians 14:5]

Examining I Corinthians 14:5 prompts us to ask why Paul said he would have liked to see all the Corinthian believers speak in tongues. As discussed during the review of verse 2 of this chapter, not all will receive this gift from the Holy Spirit. Secondly, the context of other verses proves that the tongues spoken are known human dialects spoken by various people groups. Additionally, if tongues were truly a heavenly language that ushered the speakers into the presence of God for deeper communion and holy experience, would Paul have said what he said in the second half of verse 5, that the one who prophesies is greater than one who speaks in a tongue? If speaking in tongues refers to a majestic, supernatural language spoken in heaven, is Paul saying that speaking human words of prophecy to other humans is greater than speaking with a supernatural language directly to God? And the whole church said, "No way!"

So what did Paul mean when he wrote the words of I Corinthians 14:5? As we continue reading in context, the Bible will answer the Bible and bring clarity, confidence, and conviction of God's truth.

> Now, brothers, if I come to you and speak in tongues, what good will I be to you, unless I bring you some revelation or knowledge or prophecy or word of instruction? Even in the case of lifeless things that make sounds, such as the flute or harp, how will anyone know what tune is being played unless there is a distinction in the notes? Again, if the trumpet does not sound a clear call, who will get ready for battle? So it is with you. Unless you speak intelligible words with your tongue, how will anyone know what you are saying? You will just be speaking into the air. [I Corinthians 14:6-9]

In the six verses above, Paul states without equivocation that speaking in tongues must be associated with bringing either revelation, knowledge, prophecy, or instruction to hearers. If not, as made clear in verses 7-9 (syncing with I Corinthians 13:1), the words spoken will be unprofitable among the hearers. Note: The gift of tongues is only required to be used in the sharing of God-inspired words of revelation, knowledge, prophecy, or instruction *if* the hearers speak another language not known by the speaker(s)—as was the case at Pentecost [Acts 2:5-12]. So let's dig deeper to find out why Paul spoke in tongues and desired the Corinthians to do so — with the proper motivations and a clear biblical understanding of its purpose.

In I Corinthians 14:5, Paul told the Corinthians that he would like all of them to speak in tongues as they followed his pattern for purposeful living in reaching the lost for Christ. From the Scriptures covered thus far in this book, as well as the book of Acts, we know that the apostle Paul was handpicked (appointed) by Jesus to be his "chosen instrument to carry [his] name before the Gentiles and their kings..." [Acts 9:15]. Fulfilling Jesus' prophetic words and call on his life, Paul subsequently traveled to many new regions that he had never visited before coming to know Jesus as Savior. Traveling to these places, he presented the truth of God's Word to the natives in their very own languages.

While carrying out his assignment as an apostle, evangelist, preacher, and teacher to the Gentiles, Paul spoke in tongues to various people who did not speak the languages in which he had been trained: Hebrew, Aramaic, Latin, or Greek. Beyond the wonder of being able to speak in other languages, Paul experienced overwhelming joy as he utilized the gift of tongues to communicate the gospel of Jesus Christ. His joy was not because of the gift of tongues itself but, rather, the resulting joy of seeing those previously trapped in spiritual darkness come to the saving knowledge of Jesus by hearing the message of salvation and believing in him.

Paul's joy was rooted in the salvation of those to whom he was sent, and he wanted others to be able to share in the ministry of evangelizing unreached people groups with the preaching and teaching (prophesying) of God's Word. The driver here is not the gift; it is the motivation to exalt Jesus—the Living Word—and see people saved. Paul made it clear that his desire was not for the Corinthians to merely speak in other languages. There is no glory in that. Rather, he said that in a congregational setting, believers should present God's truth (prophecy) in intelligible words that everyone can understand.

For anyone still confused about whether tongues are a mysterious heavenly language or earthly languages, in I Corinthians 14:10, Paul states again with no ambiguity that the tongues he's been referring to are "all sorts of languages in the world":

> Undoubtedly there are all sorts of languages in the world, yet none of them is without meaning. If then I do not grasp the meaning of what someone is saying, I am a foreigner to the speaker, and he is a foreigner to me. So it is with you. Since you are eager to have spiritual gifts, try to excel in gifts that build up the church. [I Corinthians 14:10-12]

He reiterates that anyone who does not grasp what someone else is saying is like a foreigner to the speaker because the words spoken are unintelligible to the listener. Again he gives the same summary statement, admonishing the Corinthian believers to eagerly engage in spiritual gifts that build up the church rather than bring confusion.

Chapter Fifteen

Edify Believers and Evangelize the World

For this reason anyone who speaks in a tongue should pray that he may interpret what he says. For if I pray in a tongue, my spirit prays, but my mind is unfruitful. So what shall I do? I will pray with my spirit, but I will also pray with my mind; I will sing with my spirit, but I will also sing with my mind. If you are praising God with your spirit, how can one who finds himself among those who do not understand say "Amen" to your thanksgiving, since he does not know what you are saying? You may be giving thanks well enough, but the other man is not edified. [I Corinthians 14:13-18]

As a reminder, in I Corinthians 12:30, Paul asked three rhetorical questions, which are all answered with an emphatic "No":

Do all have gifts of healing? Do all speak in tongues? Do all interpret?

We've learned from the Scriptures that spiritual gifts are distributed to believers by the Holy Spirit so that each person is equipped to fulfill their purpose in edifying the body of Christ and reaching the lost. We know from both I Corinthians 12:30 and I Corinthians 14:13-17 that the spiritual gift of interpreting tongues is different than the spiritual gift of supernaturally speaking in unknown languages. Thus, the Bible clarifies that not all who can speak in tongues can interpret, and vice versa. This gives us the context of what Paul is saying in I Corinthians 14:13-17.

If God gave me the gift of speaking in Polish, it would be for the express purpose of sharing the Gospel with the Polish people. Could I misuse this gift? Yes. I could sing in church with that language among others who don't know Polish and would be a major distraction from a purposeful worship experience. Without the gift of interpretation, I myself wouldn't even know what I'm saying. So why would I or anyone else (e.g., the Corinthians) do this? One major reason is pride—the very sin that infected Satan's heart and mind, causing him to rebel against God. Pride was manifesting itself in Corinthians who were using the gift of speaking in tongues to show off and desire to be the center of attention, appear uber-spiritual, and perhaps seek to manipulate others for self-gain.

Many Corinthians who were just coming out of pagan, demonically-influenced, and self-exalting religious practices were susceptible to this poisonous sin of pride. Pride and exalting oneself should not be characteristic of a true follower of Jesus Christ. Rather, the goal of Christ-followers is to exalt Jesus and walk in meekness and humility as he did during his earthly ministry. This includes the exercise of spiritual gifts.

> I thank God that I speak in tongues more than all of you. [I Corinthians 14:18]

From this verse, we see that Paul was grateful that God had given him the gift of tongues, but not because speaking in another language(s) in and of itself brought him closer to God or gave him joy, peace, fulfillment, etc. No, he was grateful for the gift because it allowed him to effectively reach unsaved people groups he could not have otherwise reached. He was overwhelmed with joy when people who had never heard the truth of God's love, grace, mercy, and redemption fell in submission/obedience to the Lord Jesus Christ.

We know from Scripture that Paul was a highly educated and learned man, trained at the feet of one of Israel's most famous scholars, Gamaliel. In one of his defenses against those boasting of their knowledge and refuting his calling as an apostle of Jesus Christ, Paul states:

> If someone else thinks they have reasons to put confidence in the flesh, I have more: circumcised on the eighth day, of the people of Israel, of the tribe of Benjamin, a Hebrew of Hebrews; in regard to the law, a Pharisee; as for zeal, persecuting the church; as for righteousness based on the law, faultless. [Philippians 3:4(b)-6].

Paul's education and high family standing provided him the opportunity to become proficient in four languages: Hebrew, Greek, Latin, and Aramaic. However, enabled of the Holy Spirit, he spoke in many cities, regions, and countries to people who spoke languages he did not naturally know. Below is a list of the many places Scripture indicates the apostle Paul traveled to fulfill his call to share the Good News of Jesus with the Gentiles:

- Amphipolis [Acts 17:1] → Greece
- Antioch (Pisidia) [Acts 13:14] → Turkey
- Antioch (Syria)[Acts 11:26; 13:1; 15:22; 18:22-23] →Turkey
- Antipatris [Acts 23:31] → Israel
- Apollonia [Acts 17:1] → North Macedonia
- Appian Way [Acts 28:13-15] → Italy
- Appii Forum [Acts 28:15] → Italy
- Arabia [Galatians 1:17]
- Assos [Acts 20:13] → Turkey
- Athens [Acts 17:16] → Greece
- Attalia [Acts 14:25] → Turkey
- Berea [Acts 17:10] → Greece
- Caesarea [Acts 9:30; 18:22; 21:8; 23:23] → Israel
- Cenchrea [Acts 18:18] → Corinth
- Corinth [Acts 18:1]
- Cyprus [Acts 13:4] (island)

- Damascus [Acts 9:19] → Syria
- Derbe [Acts 14:6, 16:1] → Turkey
- Ephesus [Acts 18:19] → Turkey
- Crete [Acts 27:8] → Greece (island)
- Iconium [Acts 13:51] → Turkey
- Jerusalem [Acts 9:26; 18:21; 21:11-17; 23:11] → Israel
- Lystra [Acts 14:6; 16:1] → Turkey
- Macedonia [Acts 16:10] → Balkan countries: Greece,
- North Macedonia, Bulgaria, Albania, Serbia, and Kosovo
- Malta [Acts 28:1] → island south of Italy
- Miletus [Acts 20:15] → Turkey
- Mitylene [Acts 20:14] → Greece (island)
- Myra [Acts 27:5] → Turkey
- Neapolis [Acts 16:11] → Greece
- Nicopolis [Titus 3:12, 15] → Greece
- Paphos [Acts 13:6] → Cyprus
- Patara [Acts 21:1] → Turkey
- Perga [Acts 13:13] → Turkey
- Philippi [Acts 16:12, 20:6] → Greece
- Ptolemais [Acts 21:7] → Libya
- Puteoli [Acts 28:13] → Italy
- Rhegium [Acts 28:13] → Italy
- Rome [Acts 28:16; II Timothy 1:17] → Italy
- Salamis [Acts 13:5] → Cyprus

- Seleucia [Acts 13:4] → Turkey
- Sidon [Acts 27:3] → Lebanon
- Spain [Romans 15:22-25, 28]
- Syracuse (Sicily) [Acts 28:12] → Italy
- Tarsus [Acts 9:30] → Turkey
- Thessalonica [Acts 17:1] → Greece
- Three Taverns [Acts 28:15] → Italy
- Troas [Acts 16:8; 20:6] → Turkey
- Trogyllium [Acts 20:15] → Turkey
- Tyre [Acts 21:3] → Lebanon

The gift of tongues enabled him to fulfill his calling as the apostle to the Gentiles and share the gospel of Jesus Christ with many people groups whose languages were foreign to him. By way of this supernatural gift, which the Scriptures say is a sign for unbelievers [I Corinthians 14:22], Paul preached the gospel, as the 120 did at Pentecost, and saw unsaved souls enlightened and rescued by God from the dominion of darkness and eternal damnation. Beyond learning the truth about the gift of tongues, the real question for us is whether we will walk in obedience to God and carry the gospel to others as Paul did.

Chapter Sixteen

Rules of Engagement

But in the church I would rather speak five intelligible words to instruct others than ten thousand words in a tongue. [I Corinthians 14:19]

The Word of God cannot be any clearer in the instruction of what is to occur within the congregation of believers. I Corinthians 14:19 explicitly states that when a congregation of believers is assembled, speaking in a language(s) that nobody else in the assembly knows should not be done. Rather, only intelligible words should be spoken for the common good of those assembled. Paul states, yet again, that the preaching and teaching of God's Word, along with worshiping him, are the focal points and purposes of Christians assembling in a corporate gathering. He informs the Corinthians that they should not be (1) making ecstatic and incoherent utterances, which was the pattern of the pagan practices in Corinth, or (2) speaking in languages of other nations not known by the hearers in the congregation.

> Brothers, stop thinking like children. In regard to evil be infants, but in your thinking be adults. [I Corinthians 14:20]

Note that in the verse above, Paul compared their thinking to children. He addressed some who, because of their lack of knowledge, were following others living in error. He spoke to others regarding their selfish motives, fleshly desires, and unbiblical actions. In keeping with I Corinthians 13:11, Paul stated that believers in Christ must not get ensnared in the devil's traps and be led into error.

God commands us to mature in our desires, reasoning, motives, thinking, and actions. To do this, we must grow up spiritually, having the Word of God and the Holy Spirit (Comforter/Counselor) as our supreme alliances and instructors. If we find that some of our mindsets and beliefs don't truly mesh with God's Word, then the Holy Spirit has brought us to a crossroads at which we must decide whether to hold on to our current beliefs or dare to live according to Romans 3:4: "Let God be true, and every man a liar."

Let's move on to examine verses 21 and 22 of I Corinthians 14:

> In the Law it is written: "Through men of strange tongues and through the lips of foreigners I will speak to this people, but even then they will not listen to me," says the Lord. Tongues, then are a sign, not for believers but for unbelievers; prophecy, however, is for believers, not for unbelievers. [I Corinthians 14:21-22]

In verse 21, Paul quotes prophetic words from Isaiah 28 that God gave Isaiah to speak to the hard-hearted Israelites around the year

700 BC. The prophecy foretold that through the Assyrians, the enemies of Israel and people of a different race and language (tongue), God would speak to his stubborn people as a sign that he was about to bring judgment on them. The tongue/language they spoke was not an angelic, heavenly language. It was, in fact, merely the language of the Assyrian race. In verse 22, Paul concludes that the purpose of tongues, in light of the contextual reading of verse 21, *is to be a sign for unbelievers* - used to bring attention to the reality that something miraculous from God is occurring, to get their attention, and to share the truth of God with them.

Conviction, Not Confusion

Paul provides contrasting scenarios in I Corinthians 14:23-25. He gives the Corinthians a vivid illustration of what would happen if some unbelievers attended a congregational worship time in which people were all speaking in languages (tongues) not known by the visitors.

> So if the whole church comes together and everyone speaks in tongues, and some who do not understand or some unbelievers come in, will they not say that you are out of your mind? But if an unbeliever or someone who does not understand comes in while everybody is prophesying, he will be convinced by all that he is a sinner and will be judged by all, and the secrets of his heart will be laid bare. So he will fall down and worship God, exclaiming, "God is really

among you!" [I Corinthians 14:23-25]

The purpose of all spiritual gifts is to point people to Jesus so that they will repent of their sins and be spiritually born-again, saved from the penalty and power of sin, and grow in their relationship with the Lord. This was the pattern established by the disciples to whom God first gave the gift of tongues [Acts 2:1-18], and it is what Paul states is still the pattern:

> What then shall we say, brothers? When you come together, everyone has a hymn, or a word of instruction, a revelation, a tongue or an interpretation. All of these must be done for the strengthening of the church. If anyone speaks in a tongue, two—or at the most three—should speak, one at a time, and someone must interpret. If there is no interpreter, the speaker should keep quiet in the church and speak to himself and God. Two or three prophets should speak, and the others should weigh carefully what is said. And if a revelation comes to someone who is sitting down, the first speaker should stop. For you can all prophesy in turn so that everyone may be instructed and encouraged. The spirits of prophets are subject to the control of prophets. For God is not a God of disorder but of peace —as in all the congregations of the Lord's people. [I Corinthians 14:26-33]

The purpose of all spiritual gifts is echoed again in the last sentence of verse 26. When believers come together, all actions and words "must be done for the strengthening of the church." The clear protocol for exercising the gift of tongues in a congregational setting, among both people who have trusted Christ as Savior and those who have not yet done so, is stated in verses 27 and 28 (take a moment to re-read). Verses 29-32 refer to the gift of prophecy that God has given to some in the body of Christ. Verse 33 reiterates that God is not the author of chaos and confusion. Therefore, ecstatic utterances that no one can understand and interpret are not biblical and are rejected as inappropriate. Among believers, therefore, should be only sound and intelligible preaching and teaching. If, however, tongues are spoken among believers, interpretation must also be provided, as Scripture clearly teaches.

Discussed in previous chapters were the cultural, moral, and spiritual happenings in the city of Corinth relating to the role of women in society and the rampant spiritual perversion among its inhabitants, due to demonic influence. With that in mind, let's look at the next few verses:

> Women should remain silent in the churches. They are not allowed to speak, but must be in submission, as the law says. If they want to inquire about something, they should ask their own husbands at home; for it is disgraceful for a woman to speak in the church. [I Corinthians 14:34-35]

In the verses above, Paul was not saying that women could not speak or pray in the church (re-read 11:5). Rather, he was instructing the Corinthians, many of whom having just come out of pagan rituals and practices, to forbid women to stand up and speak to the congregation and, most importantly, to not allow them to carry on the wild self-speech they used to blurt out in their former demonically-influenced cults. Furthermore, because wickedness was so widespread in Corinth, he wanted them (the Christians) to set themselves apart as reverent, orderly, and purposeful in bringing attention only to God in their church/worship services:

> Did the word of God originate with you? Or are you the only people it has reached? If anybody thinks he is a prophet or spiritually gifted, let him acknowledge that what I am writing to you is the Lord's command. If he ignores this, he himself will be ignored. Therefore, my brothers, be eager to prophesy, and do not forbid speaking in tongues. But everything should be done in a fitting and orderly way. [I Corinthians 14:36-40]

The summary of all that's been examined in chapters 12 through 14 of I Corinthians regarding the spiritual gift of tongues is this:

1. Exalt the Lord in attitudes, words, actions, and reactions.
2. Preach and teach God's Word with seriousness and soundness of doctrine and speech.
3. Use the gift of tongues (if given to you by the Holy Spirit AND is necessary) for what it was given to do: glorify God

in reaching the lost who don't speak your native language as a sign in evangelism, doing everything decently and in order.

It is my sincere hope that readers of this book will contemplate and embrace what the Scriptures illuminate as truth regarding the topics we have analyzed. Decoding the mysteries of the baptism of the Holy Spirit and speaking in tongues was the intent of this book and my prayer is that you continue to grow in faith, hope, and love – living with peace, power, and purpose as you surrender each day to the Lord Jesus Christ.

Made in the USA
Middletown, DE
02 October 2023

39820309R00076